AF505769

# JULIÃO SARMENTO

ONE HUNDRED SEVENTY ONE ENTERTAINMENT CELEBRITIES

MER.

# 1. ALMODOVAR, Pedro

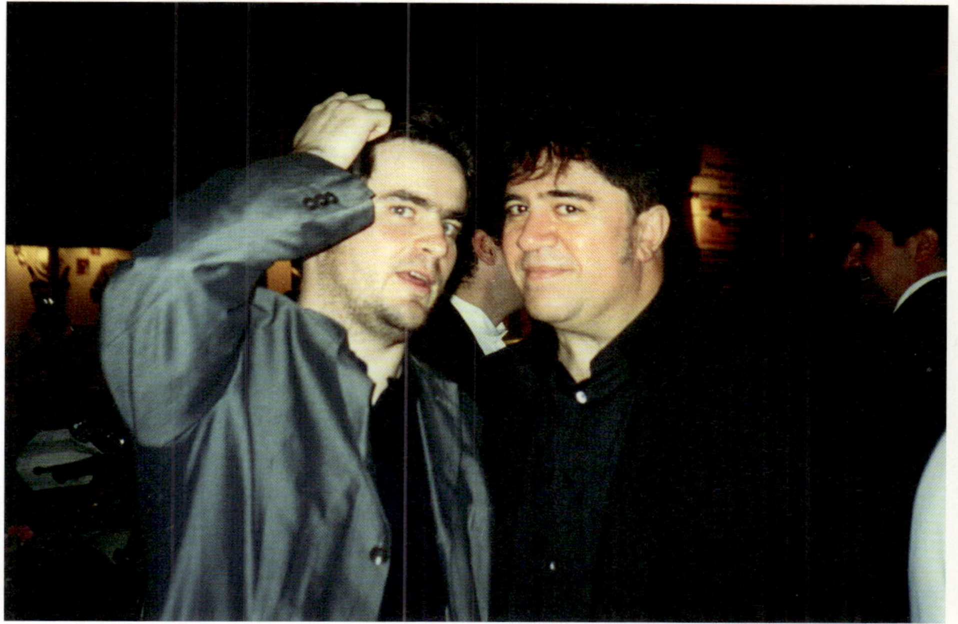

A 1

# 2. ARGENTO, Asia

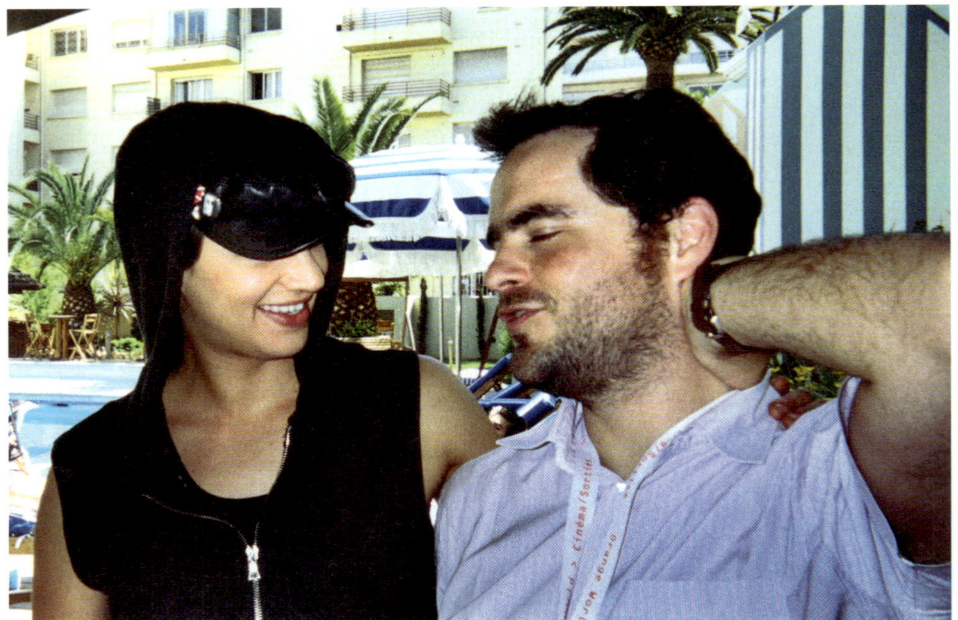

# 3. ASTIN, Sean

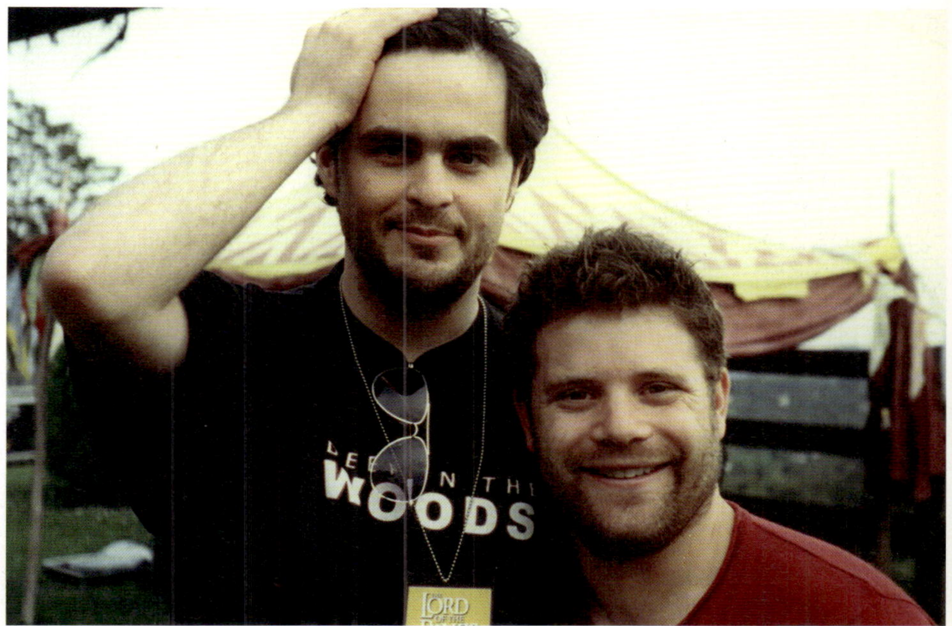

# 4. AZARIA, Hank

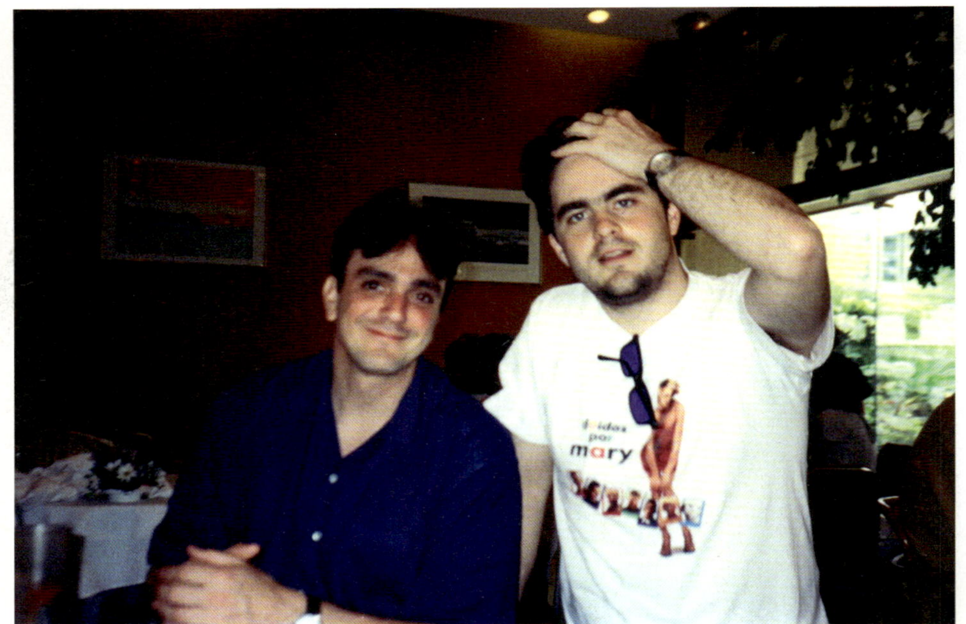

# 5. BACON, Kevin

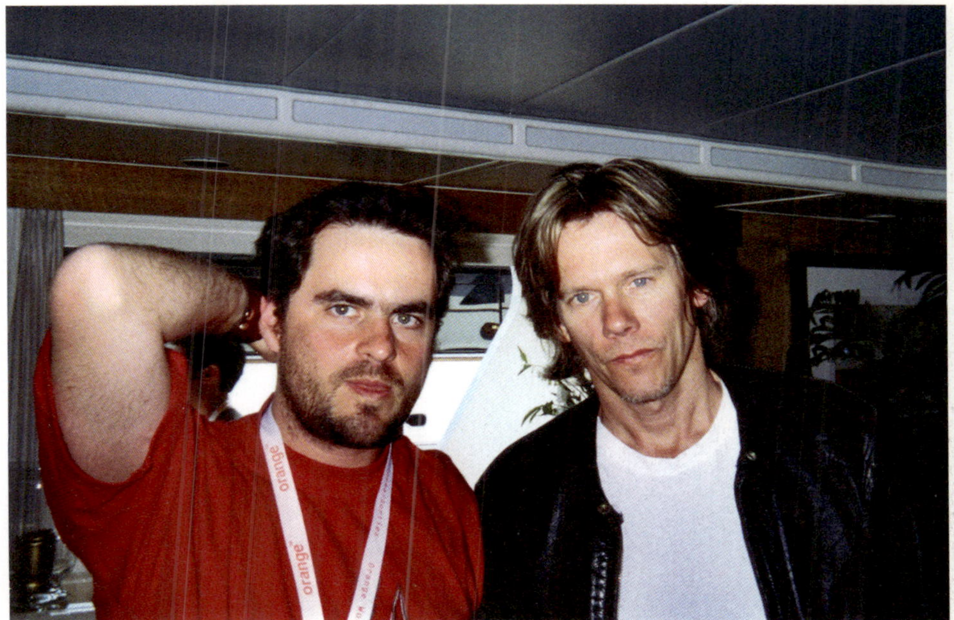

B 1

# 6. BACRI, Jean-Pierre

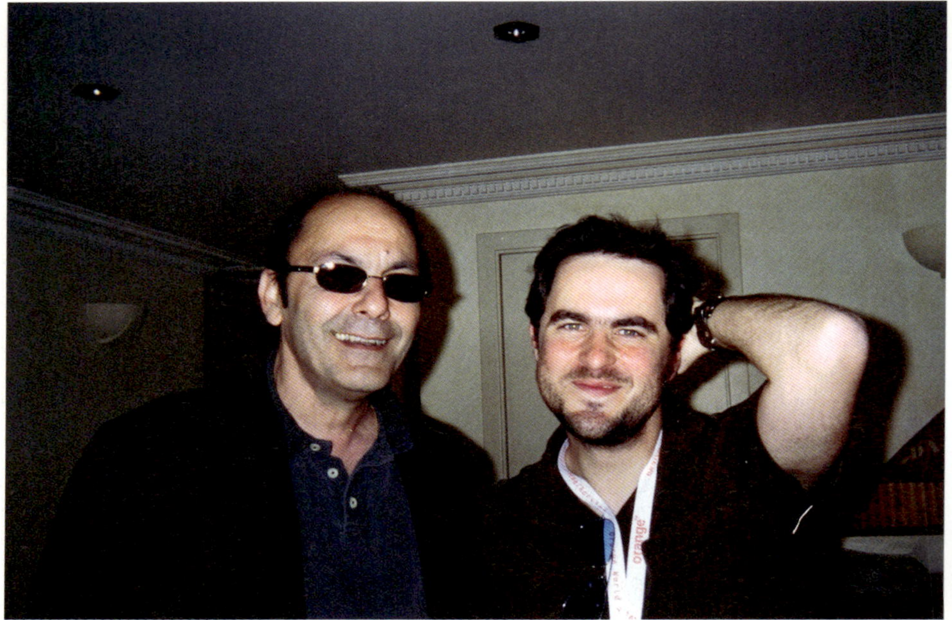

B 2

# 7. BAER, Eduard

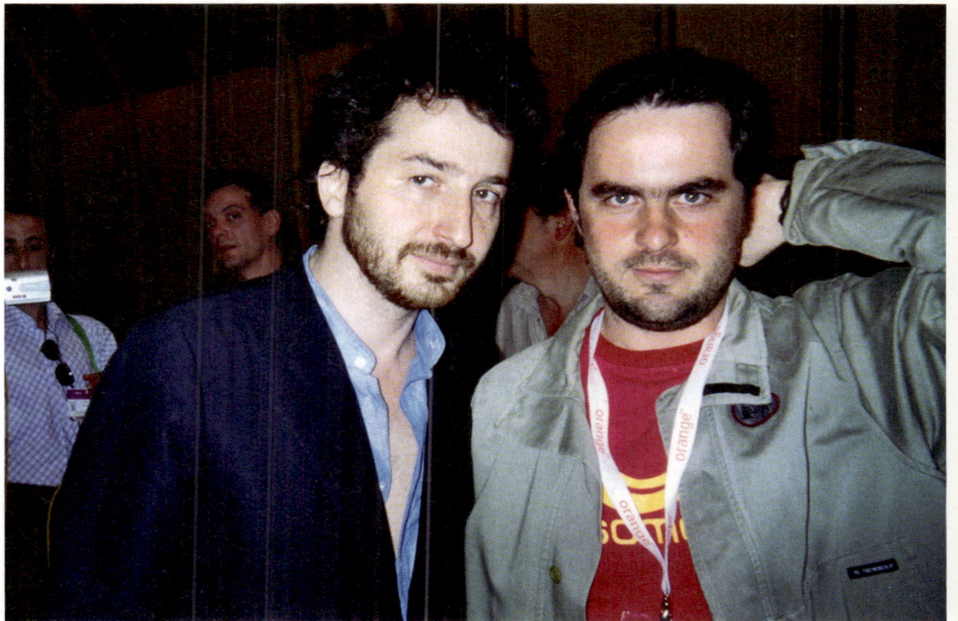

# 8. BALE, Christian

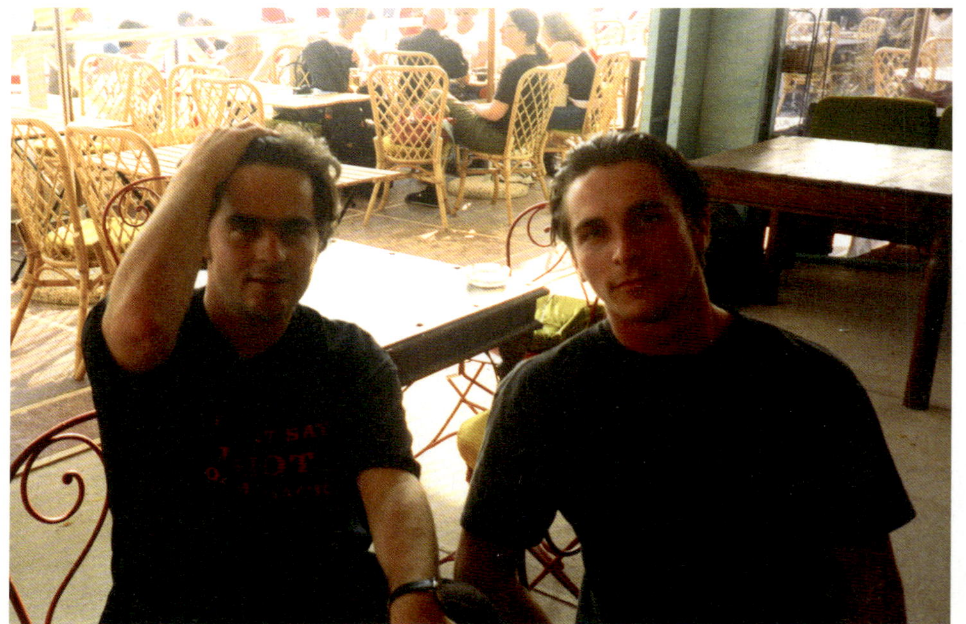

# 9. BARRYMORE, Drew

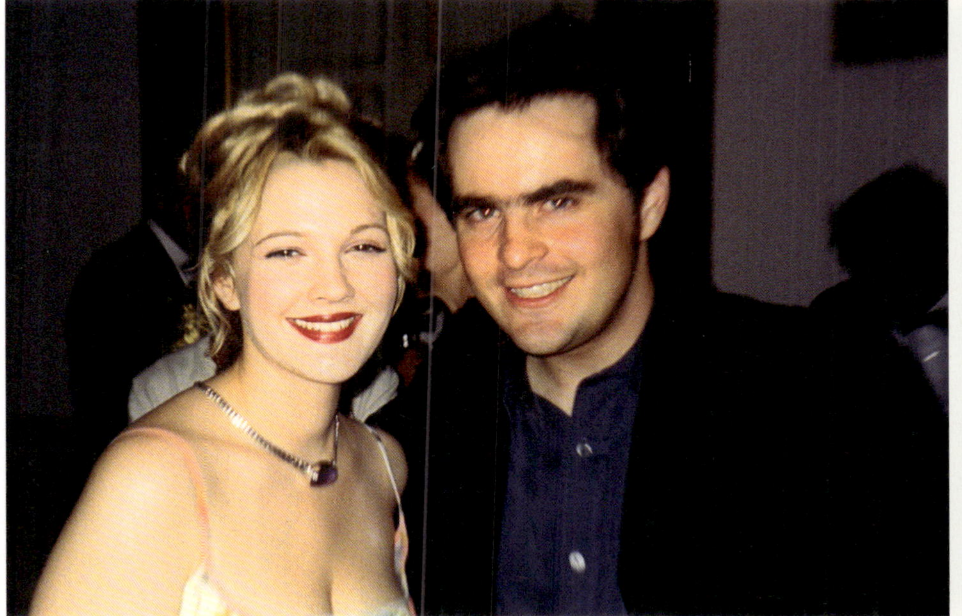

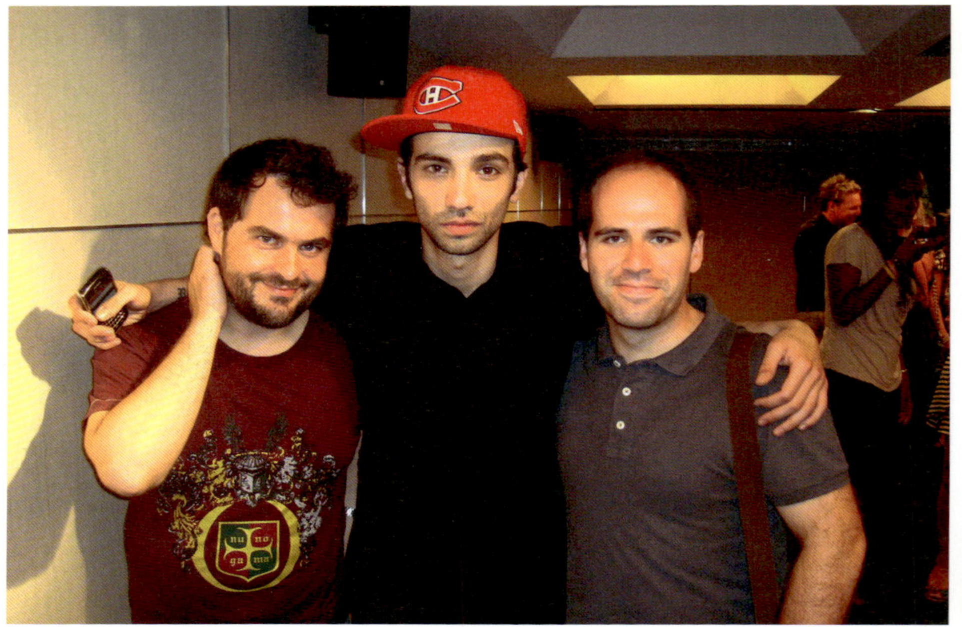

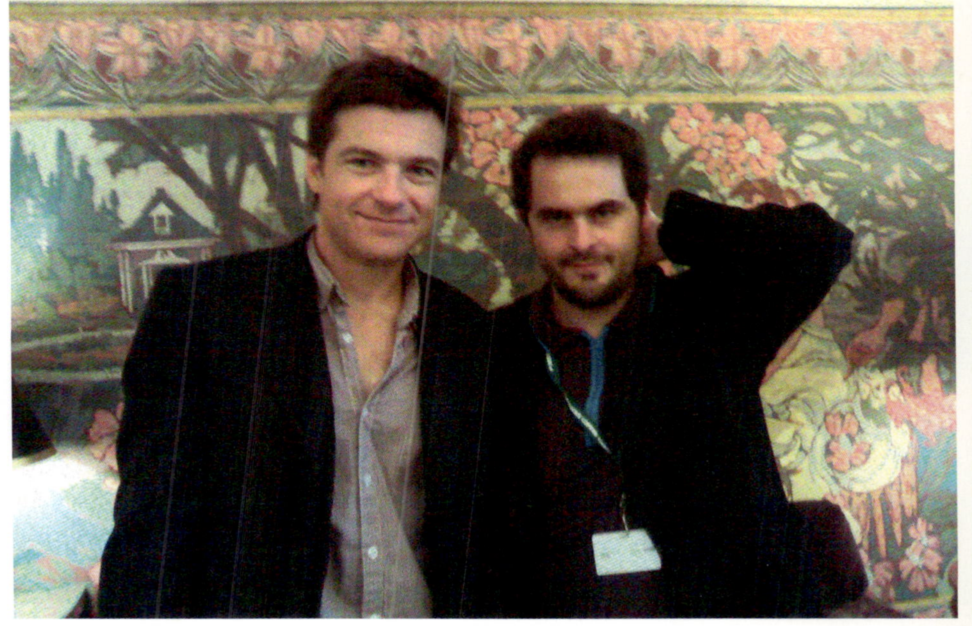

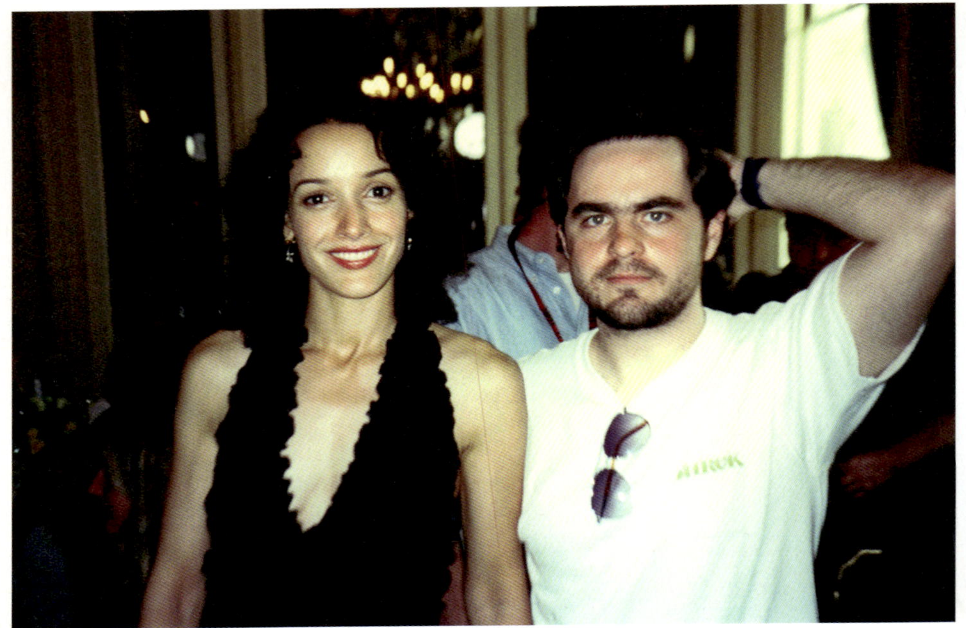
ATTACK

# 14. BELLUCCI, Monica

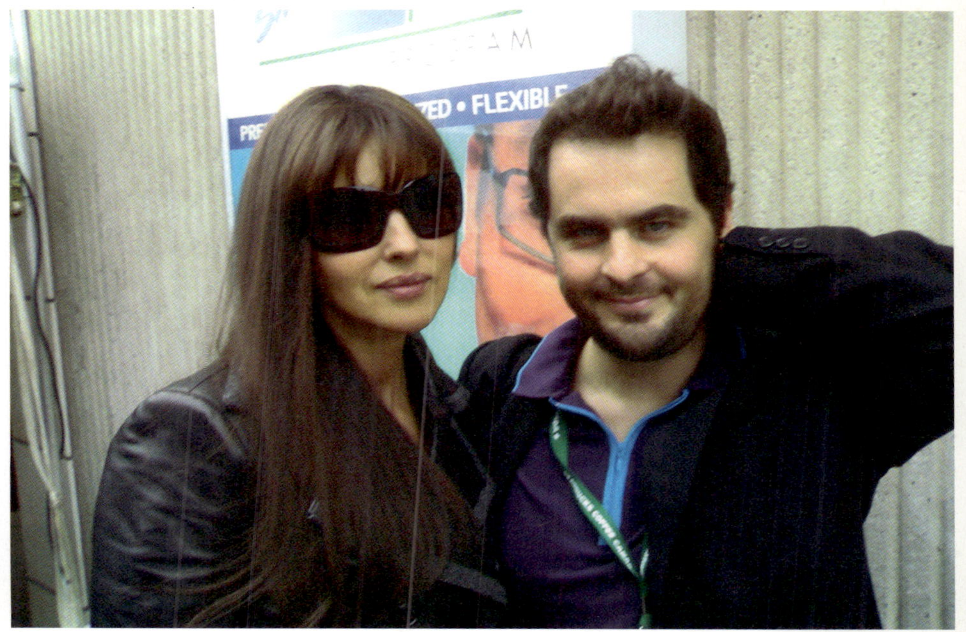

# 15. BIRCH, Thora

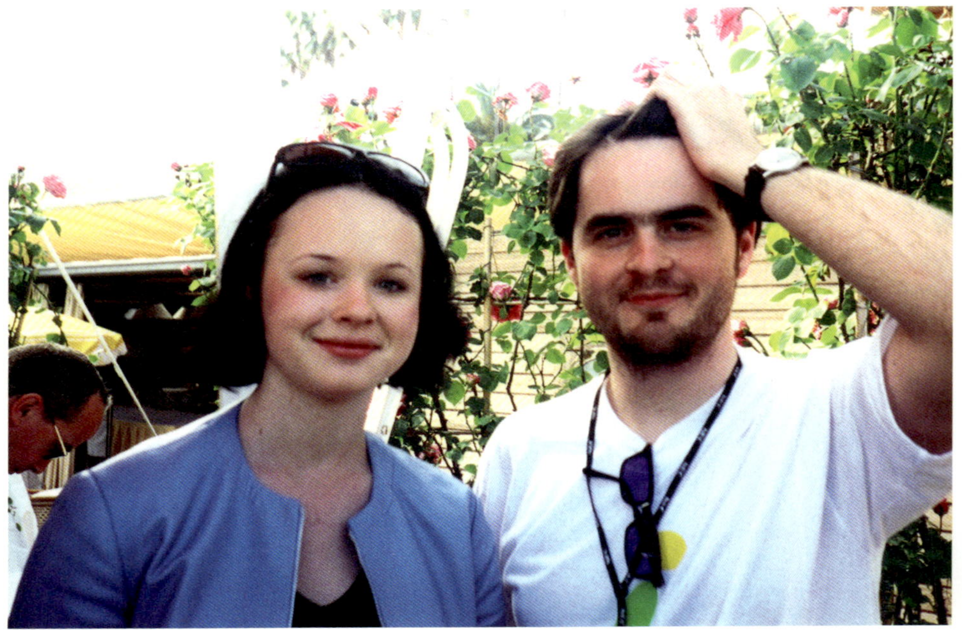

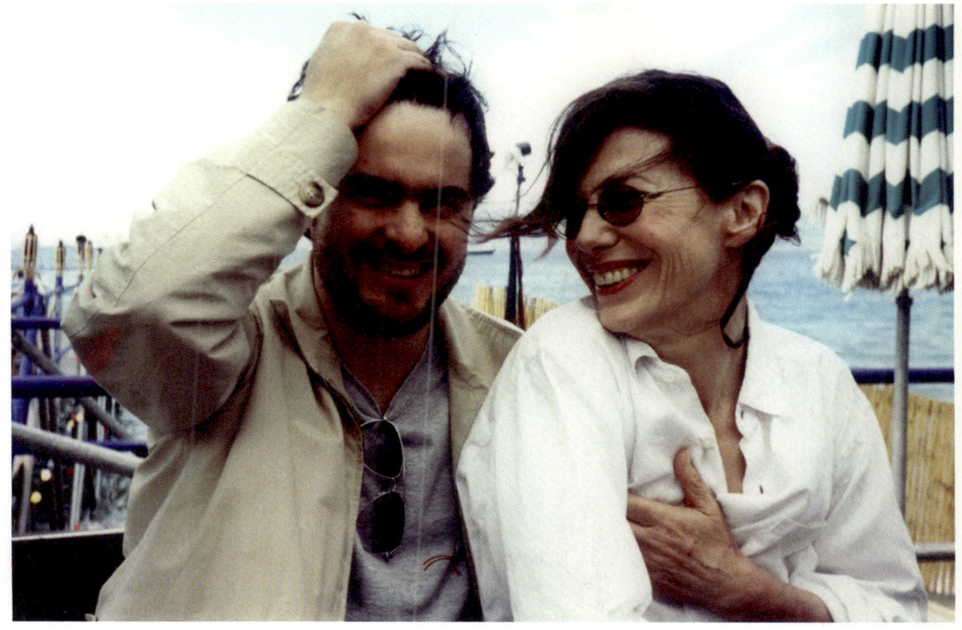

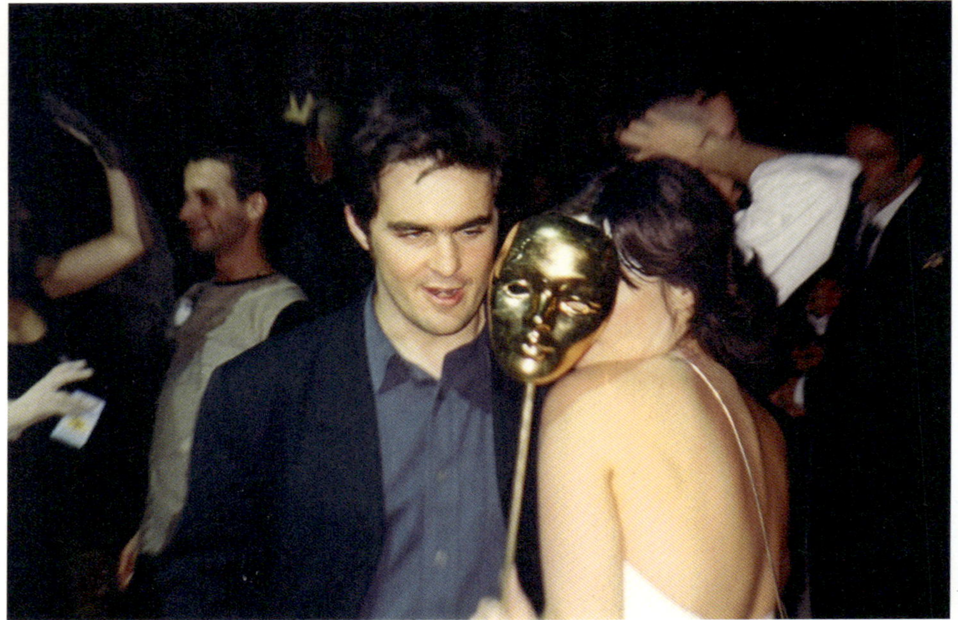

# 18. BON JOVI, Jon

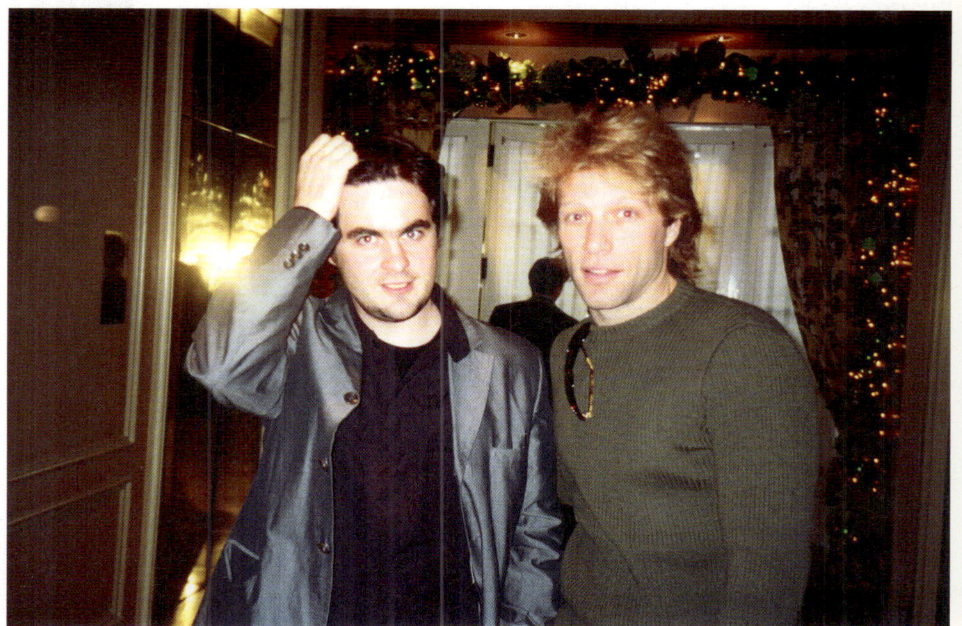

B 13

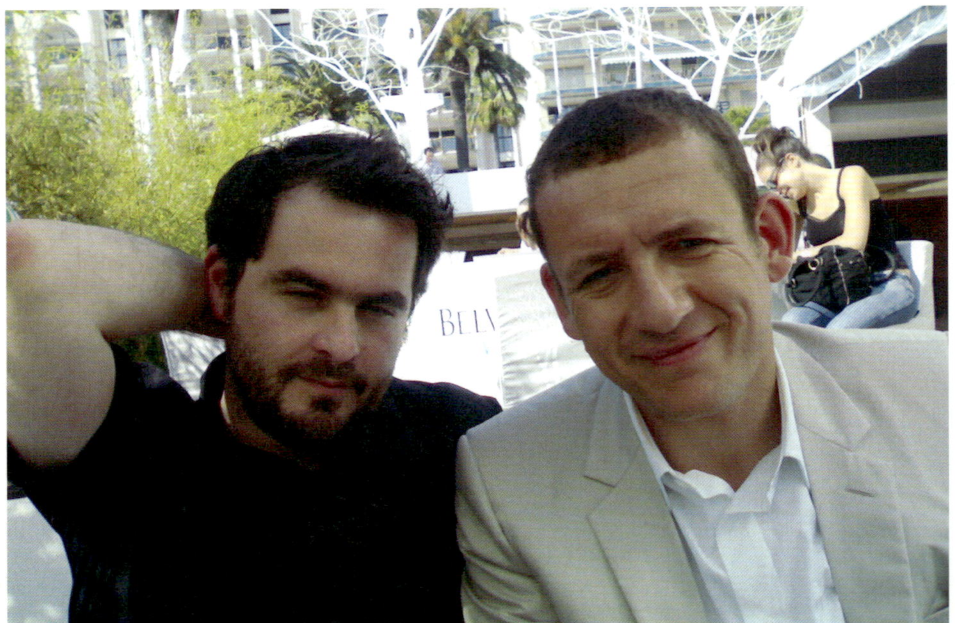

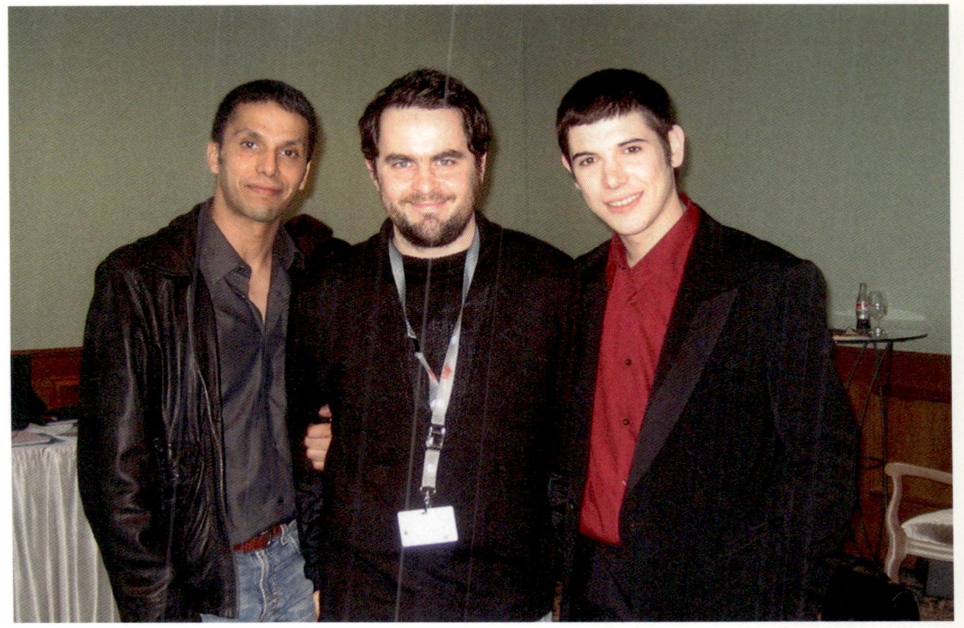

# 22. BRAGA, Alice

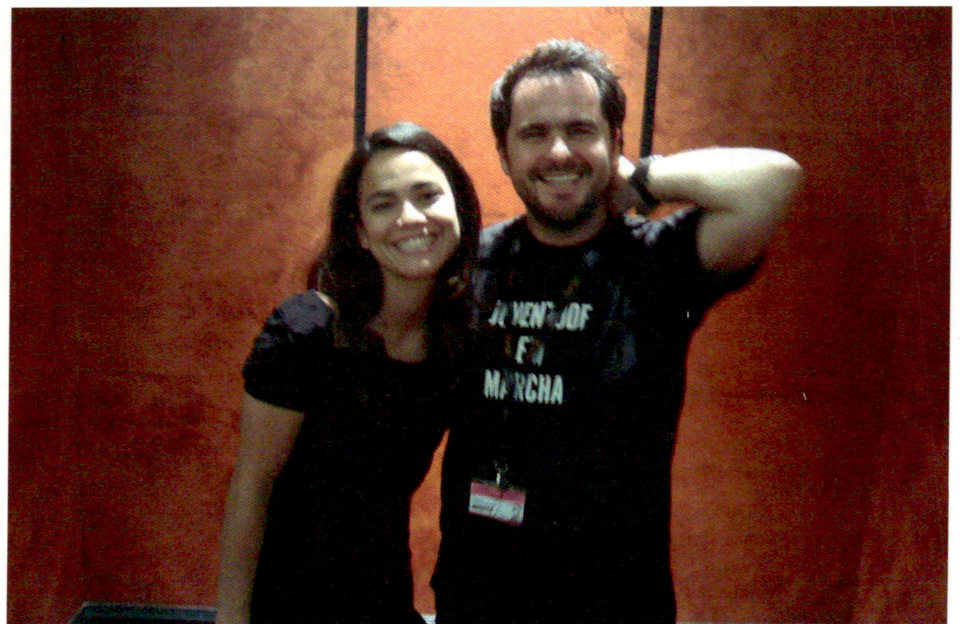

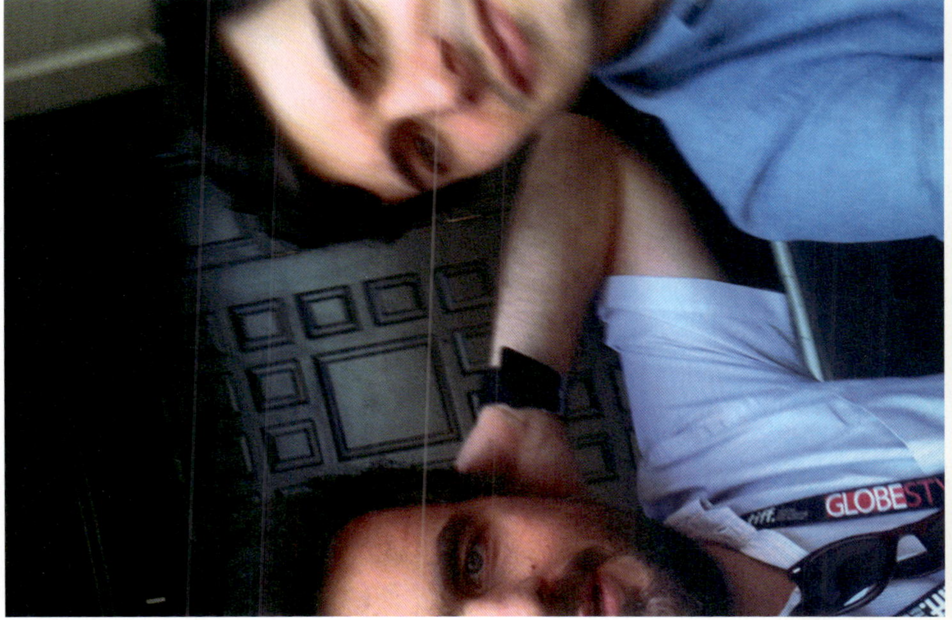

GLOBESTY

# 24. BRODY, Adrien

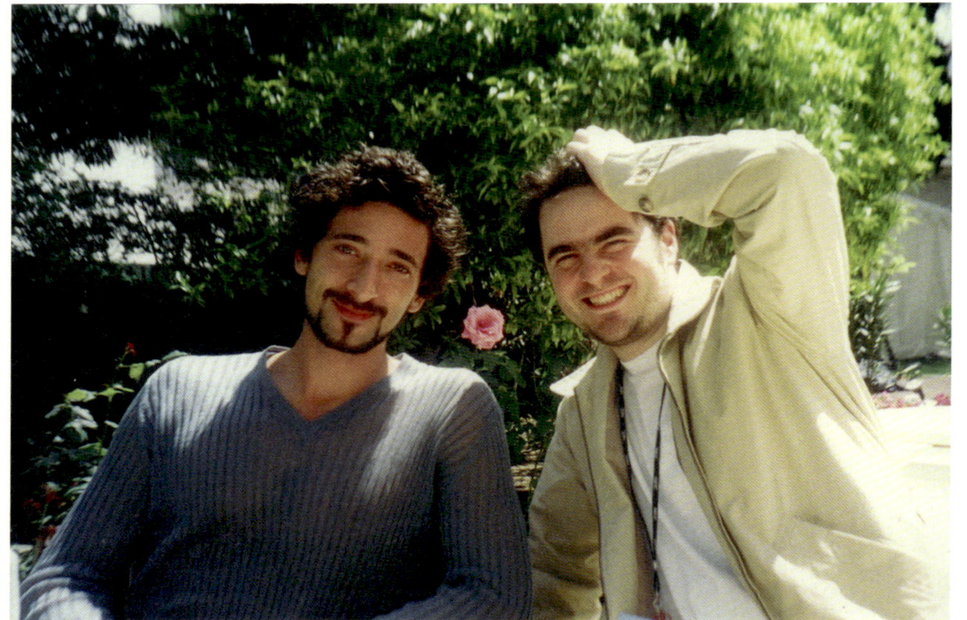

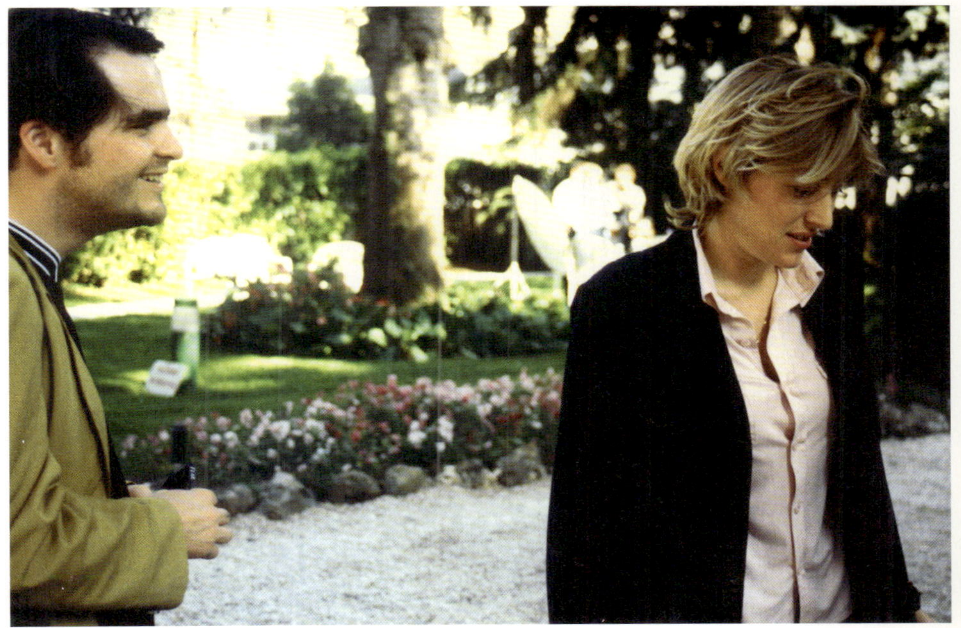

B 19

## 26. BUSCEMI, Steve

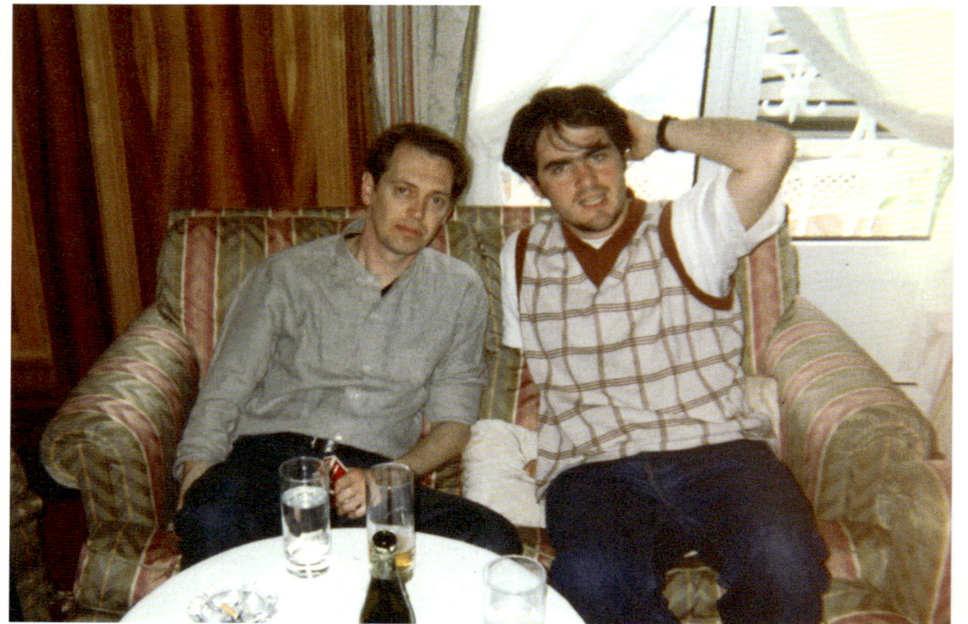

# 27. BUTLER, Gerard

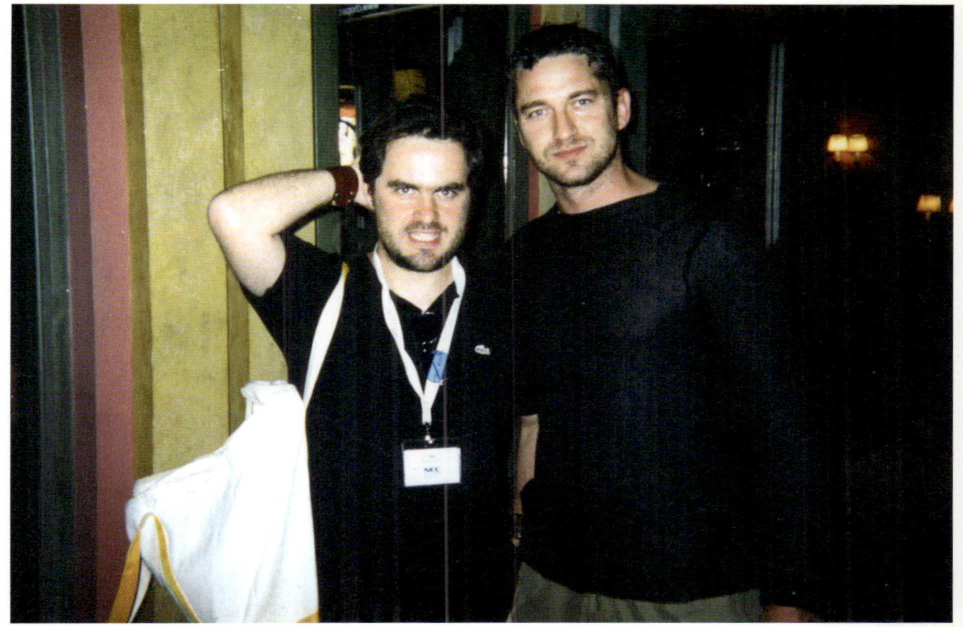

# 28. CAINE, Michael

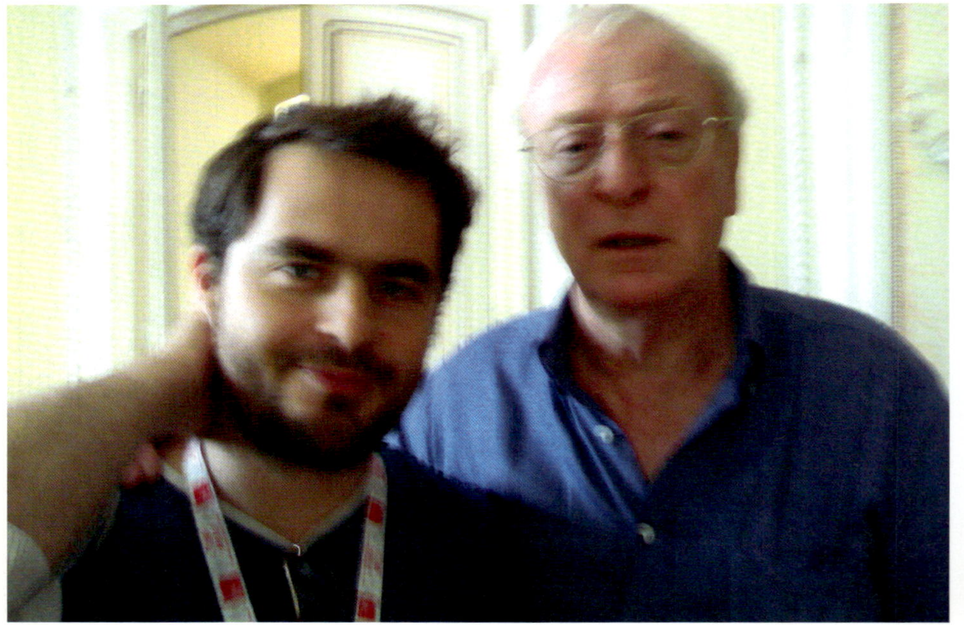

C 1

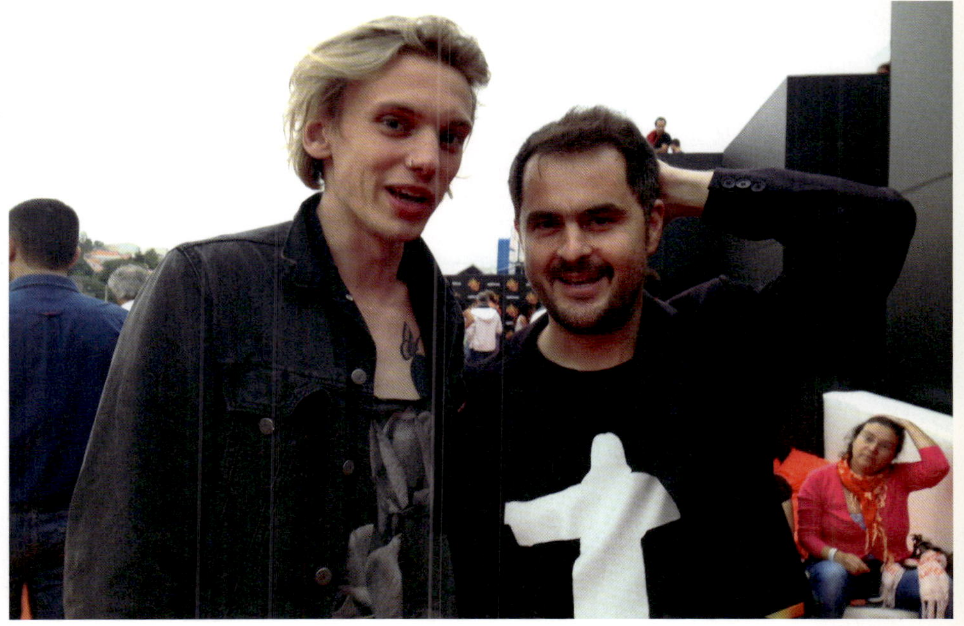

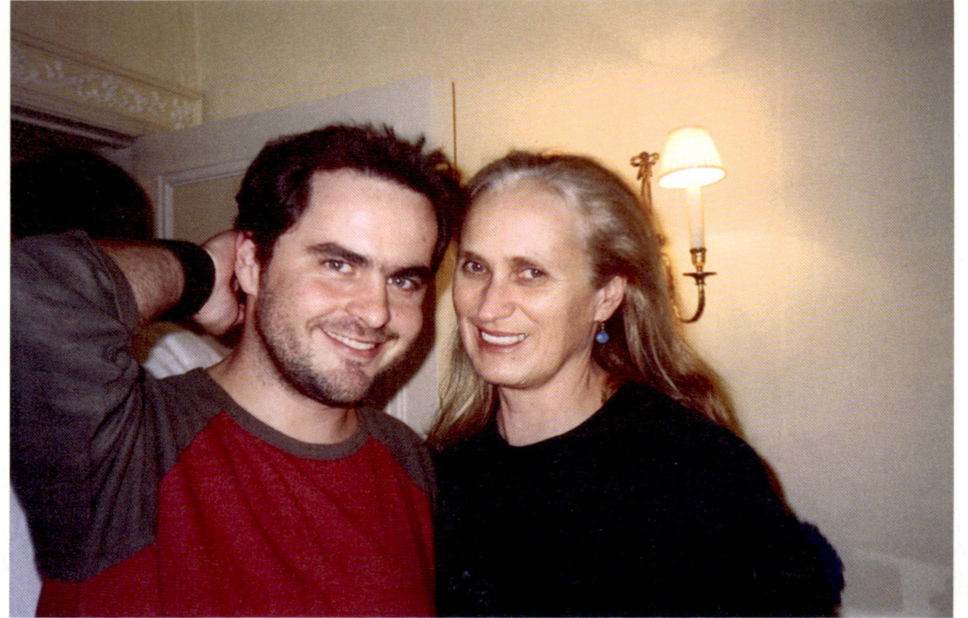

# 31. CANEÇAS, Lili

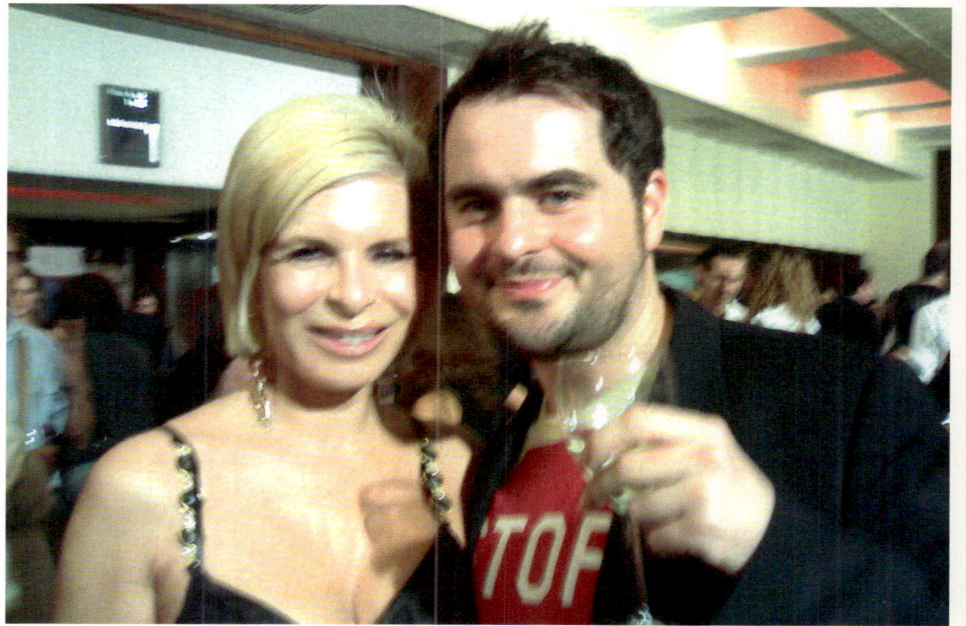

C 4

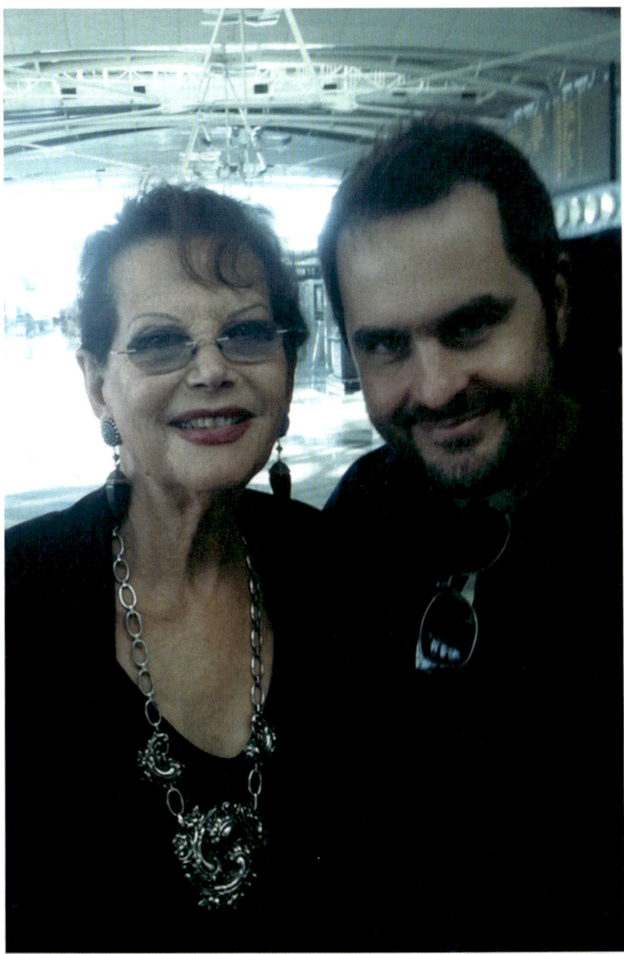

C 5

# 33. CARRADINE, David

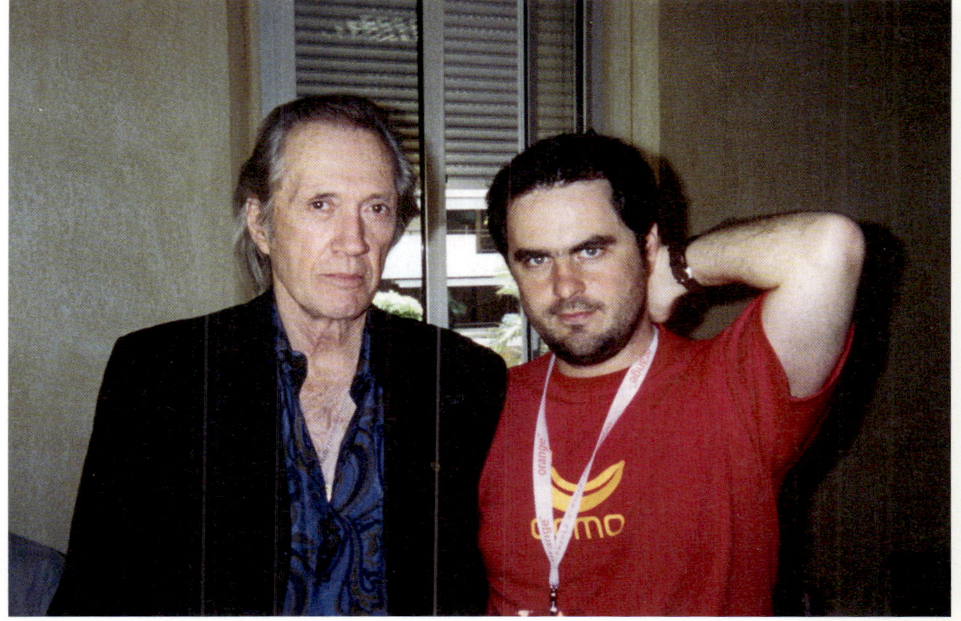

C 6

# 34. CARRÉ, Isabelle

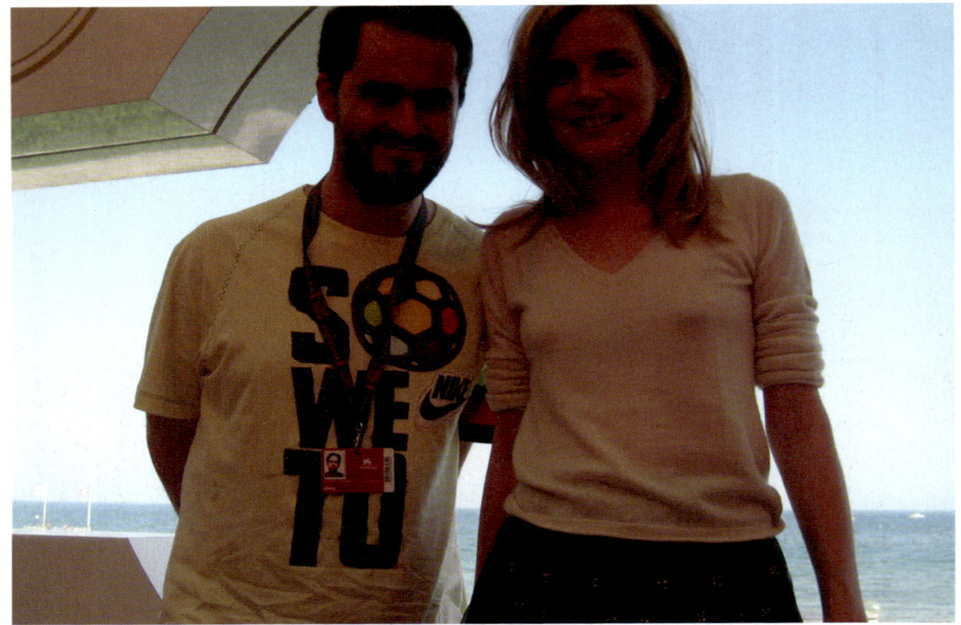

C 7

# 35. CASSEL, Vincent

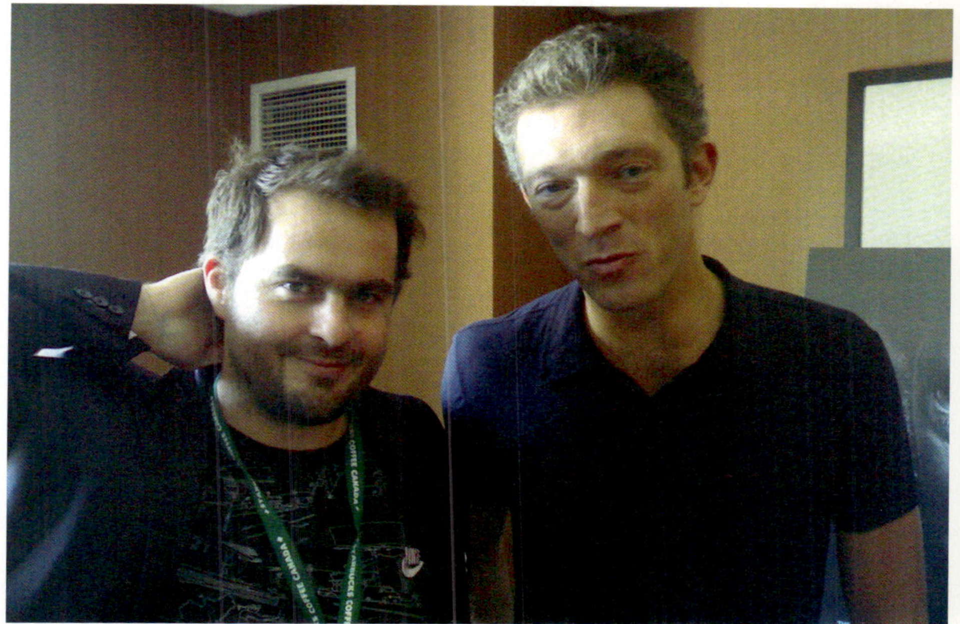

# 36. CASTELLO, Sergio

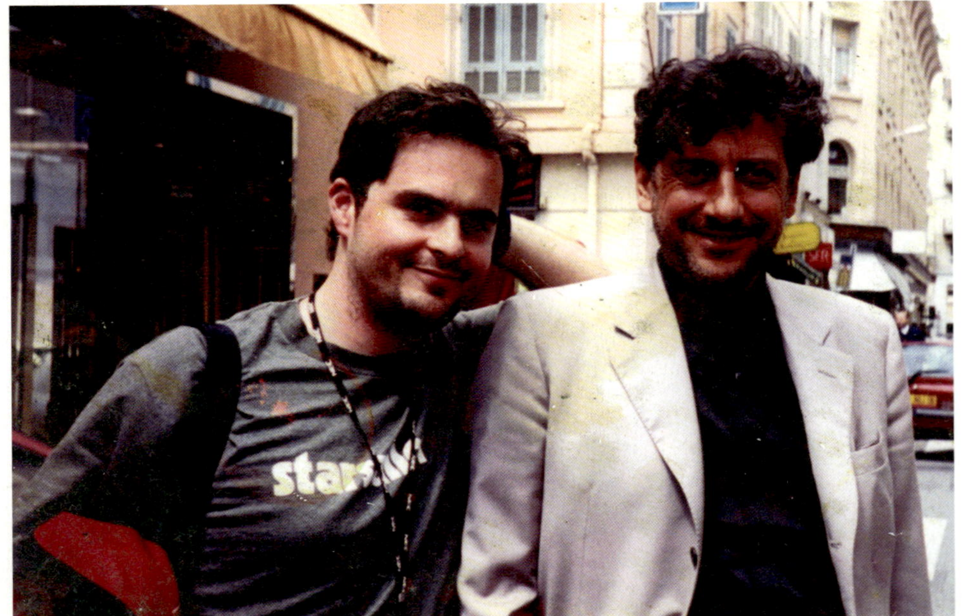

# 37. CHAVES, Soraia

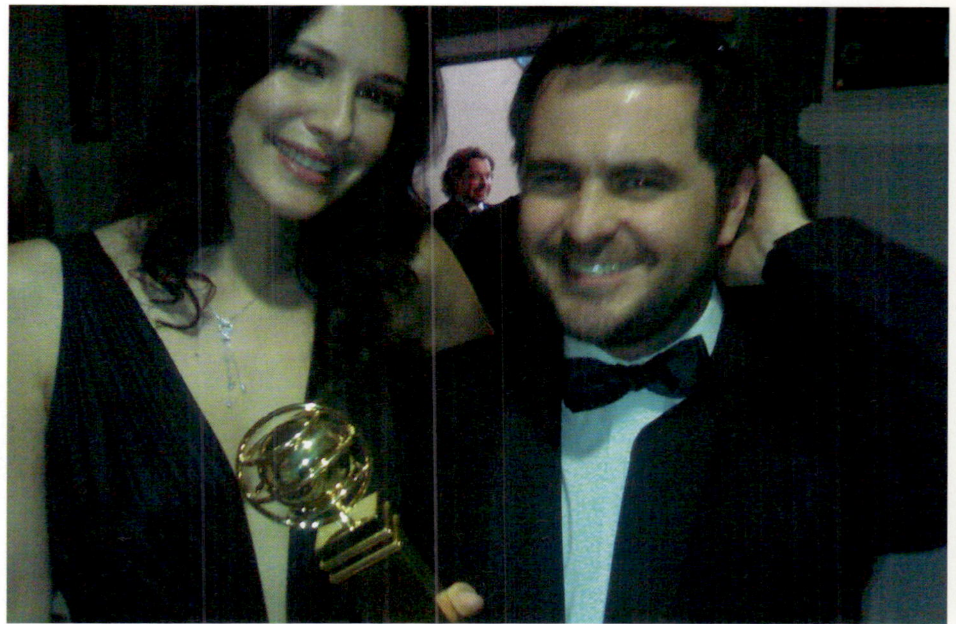

C 10

# 38. CLARK, Larry

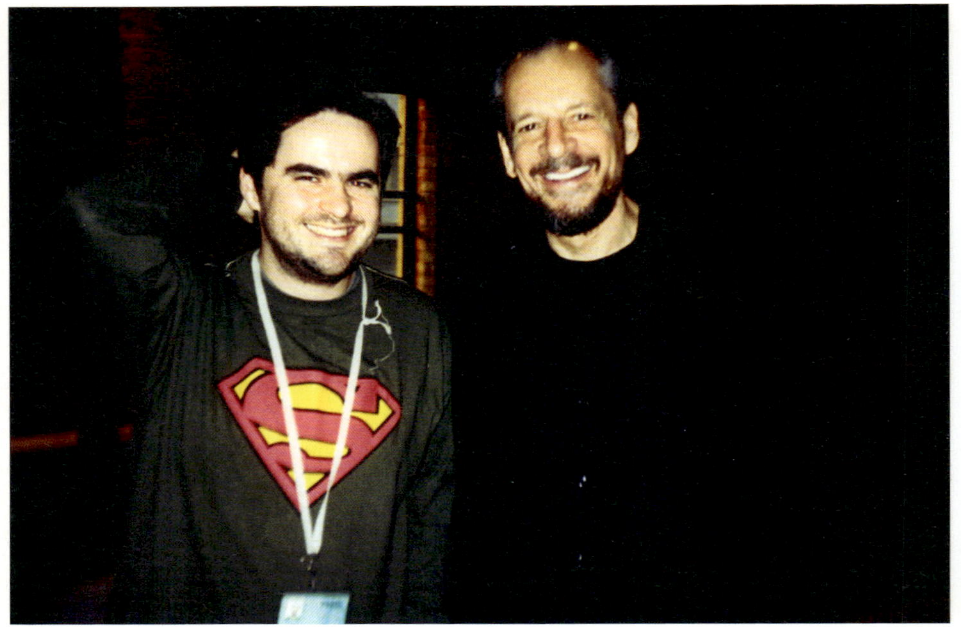

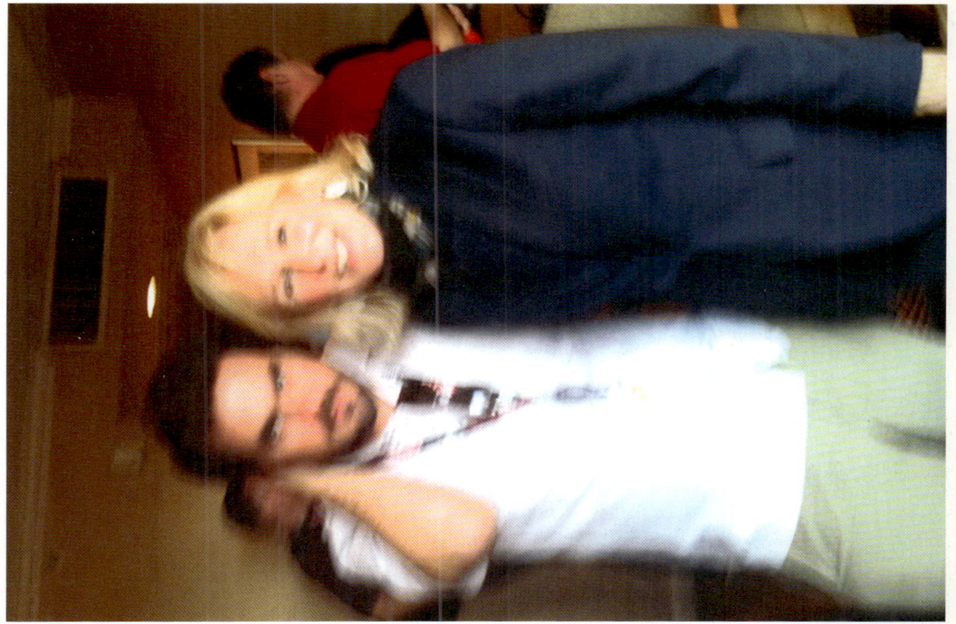

# 40. COCKER, Jarvis

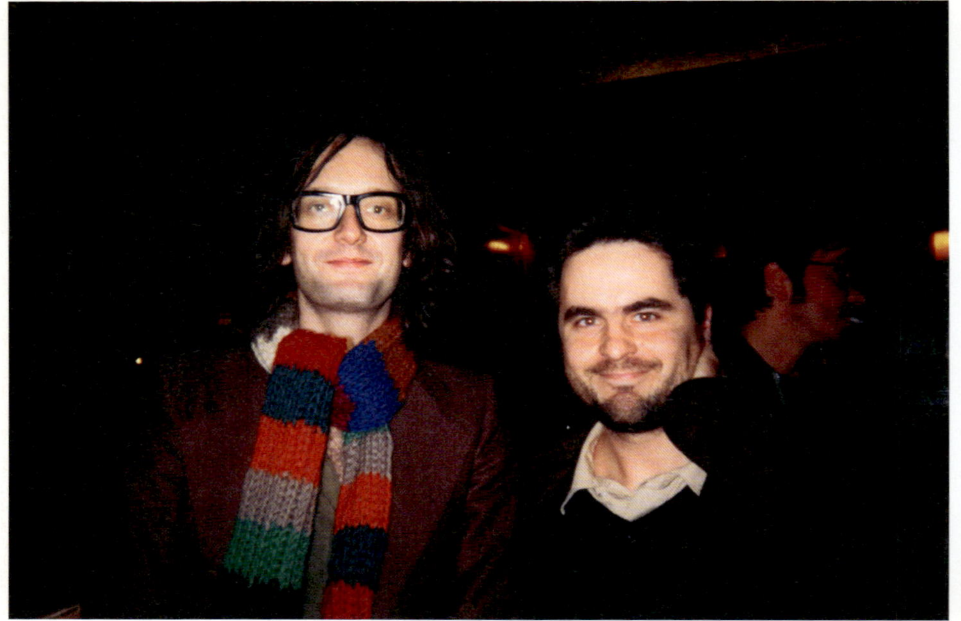

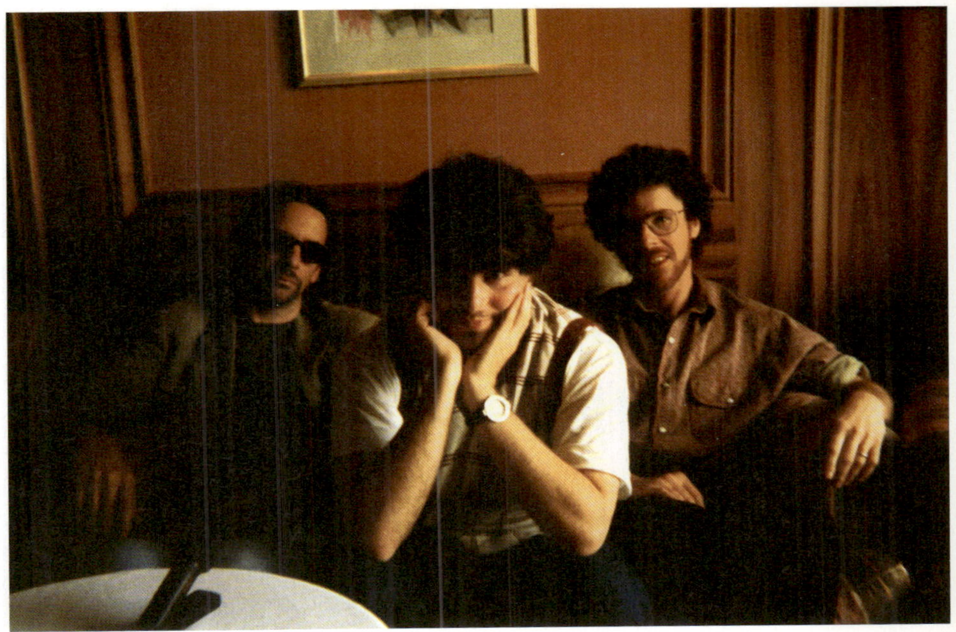

# 43. COLLETTE, Toni

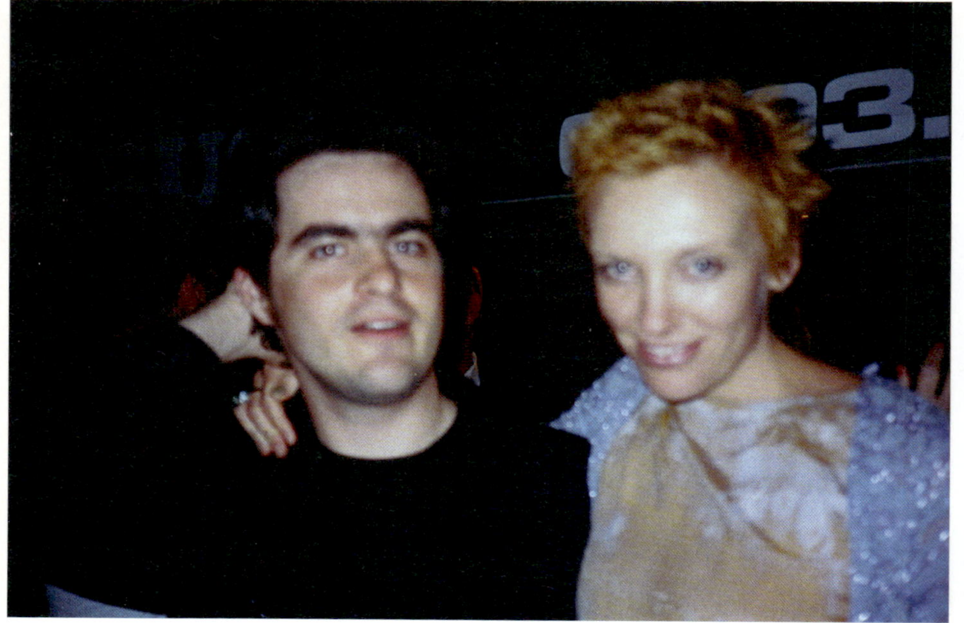

# 44. COLM, Meaney

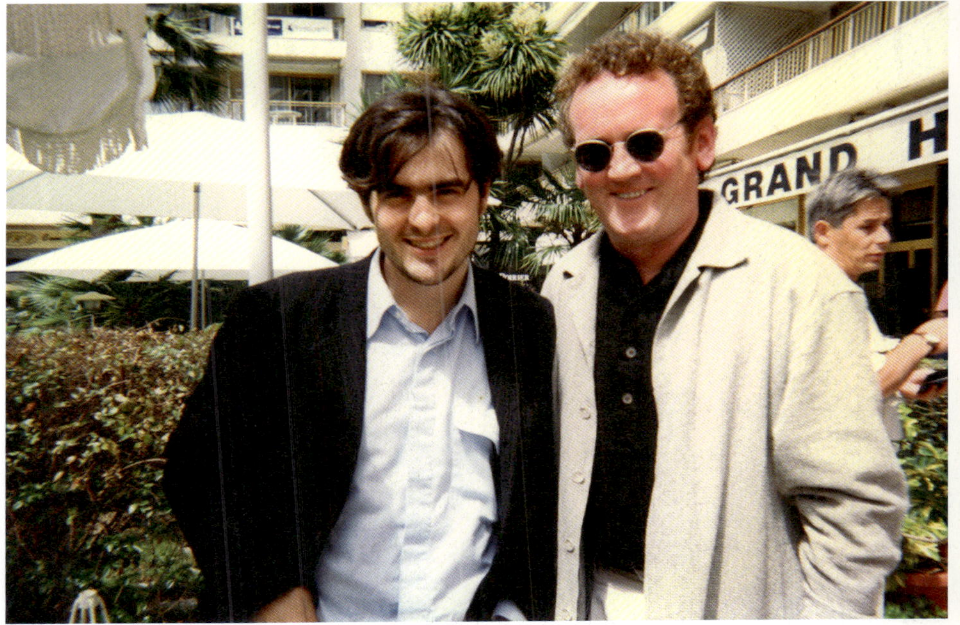

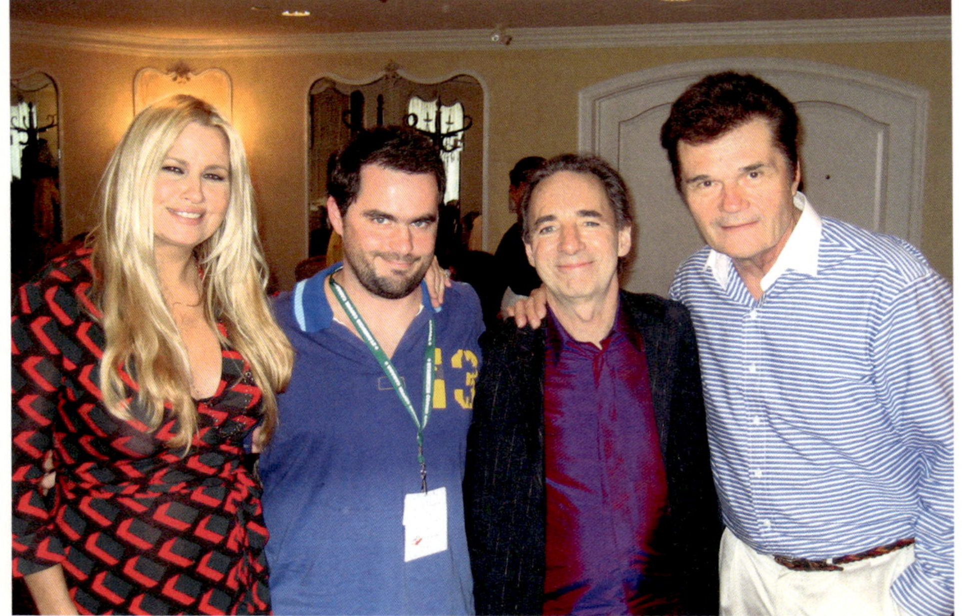



**47. WILLARD, Fred**

# 48. COPPOLA, Sofia

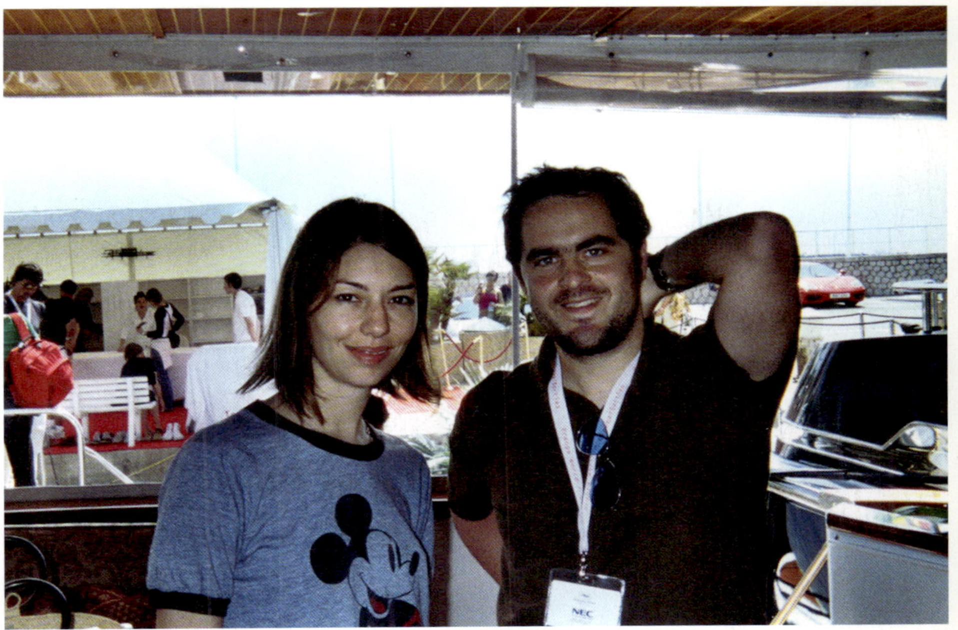

# 49. COSTNER, Kevin

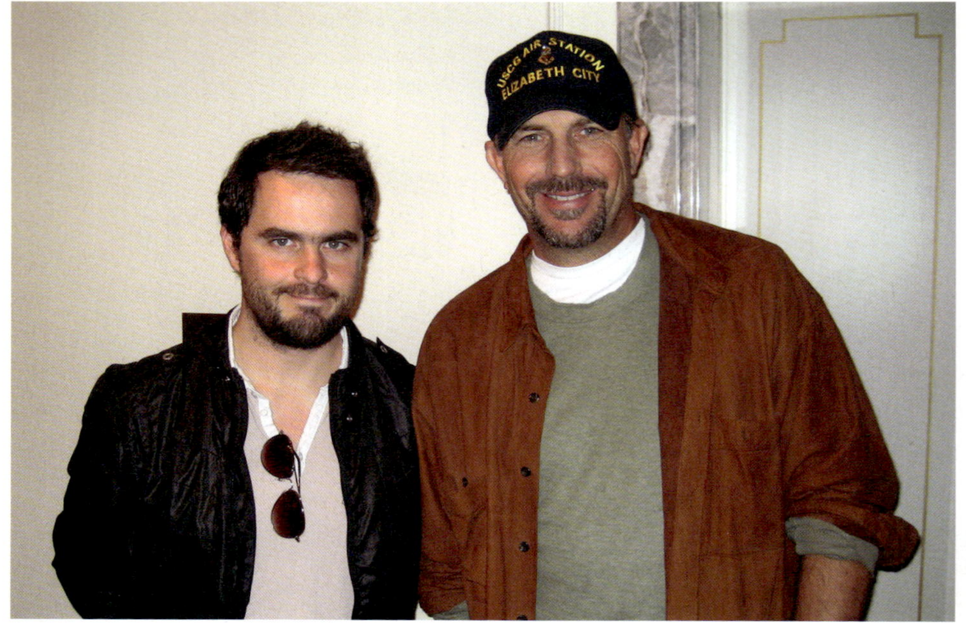


C 19

# 50. COTILLARD, Marion

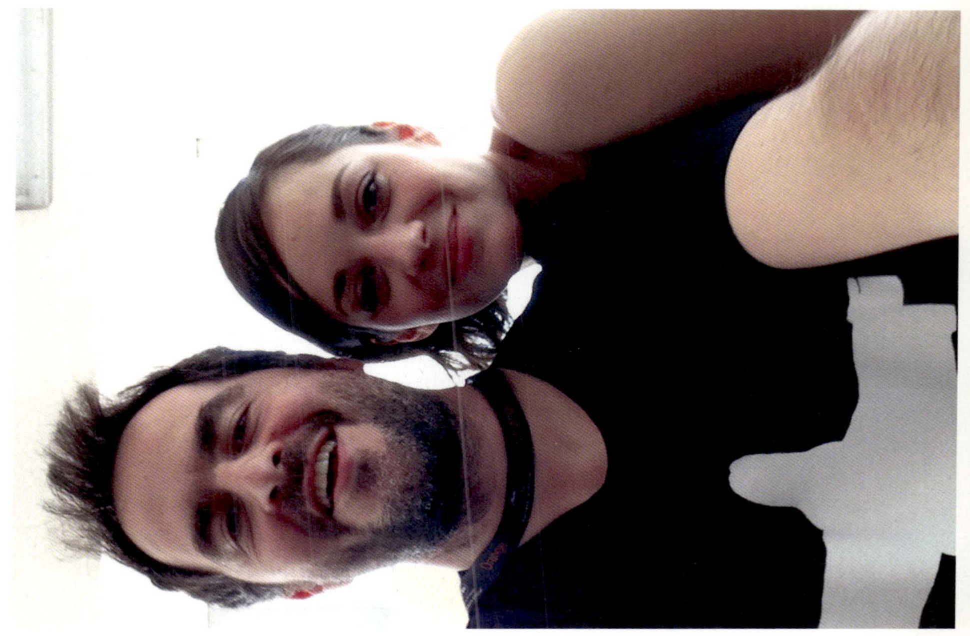

# 51. CRUZ, Penélope

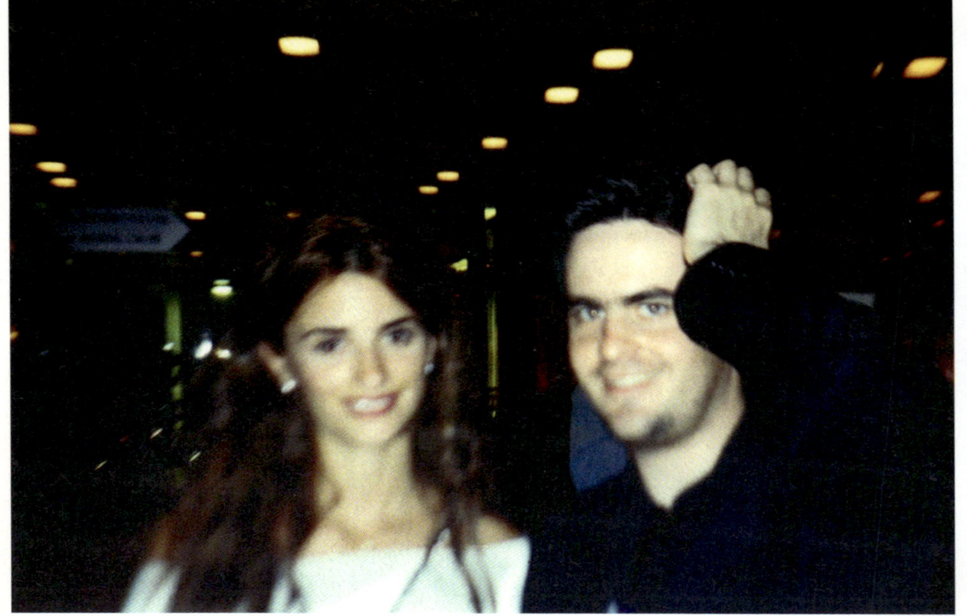

# 52. CUMBERBATCH, Benedict

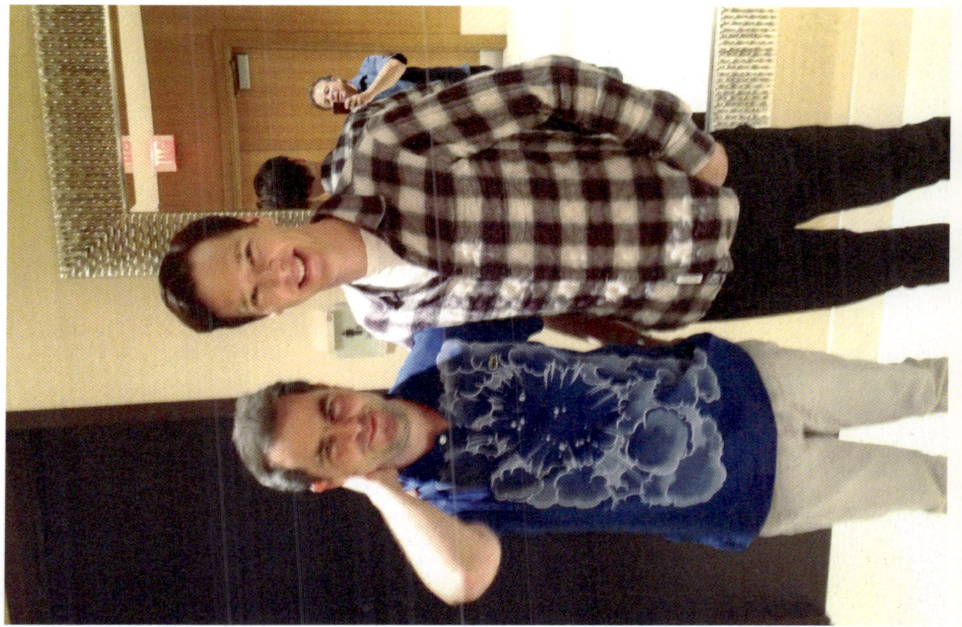

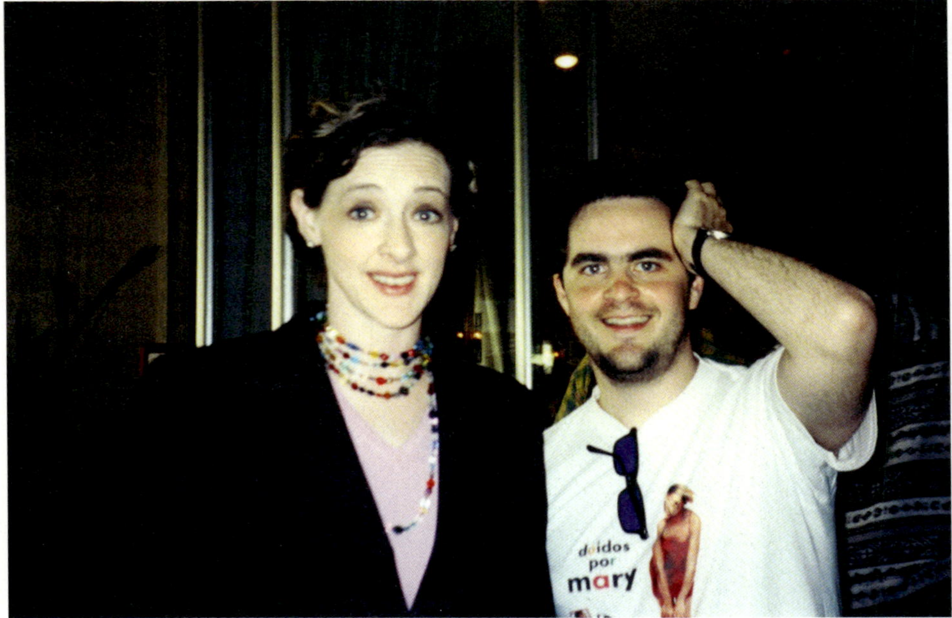

# 54. DAVIS, Hope

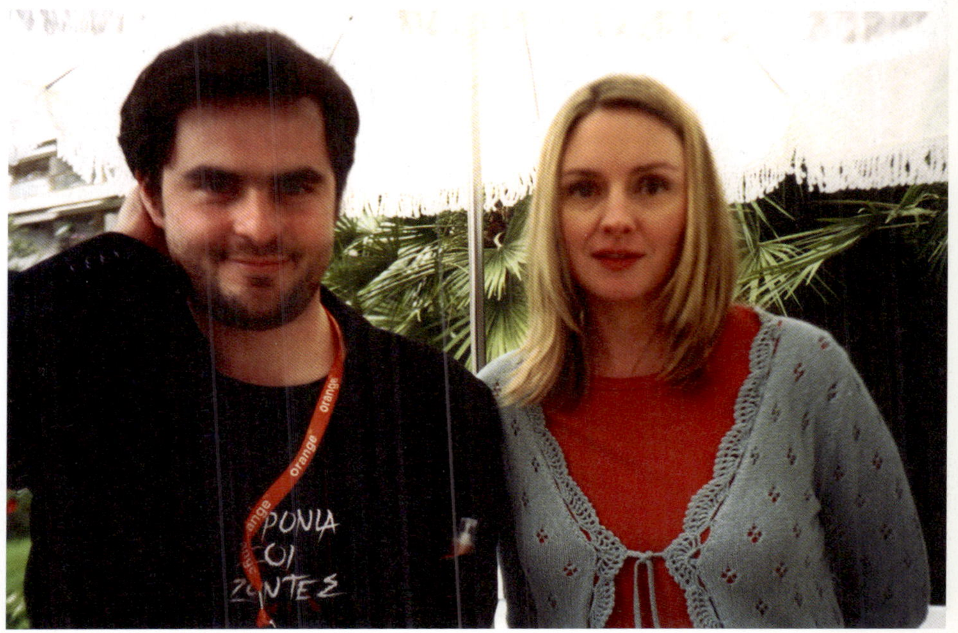



D 1

# 55. DE ALMEIDA, Joaquim

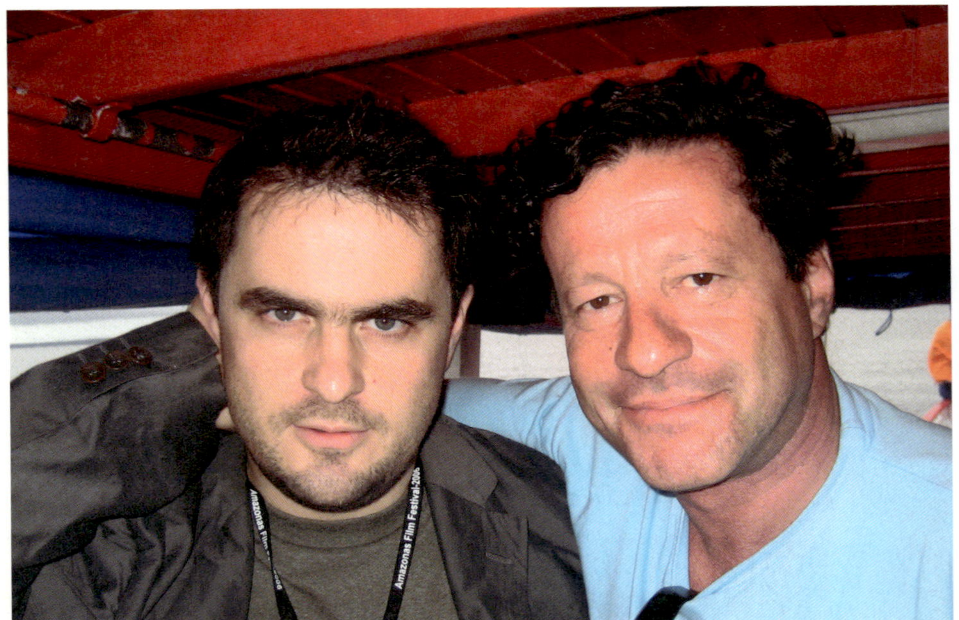

D 2

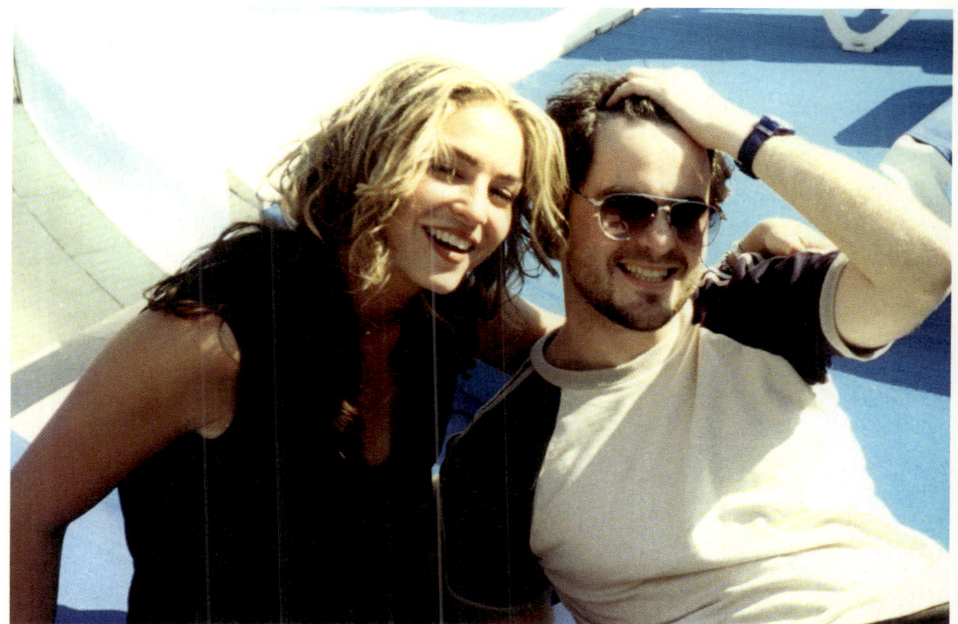

## 56. DE MATTEO, Drea

D 3

# 57. DE OLIVEIRA, Manuel

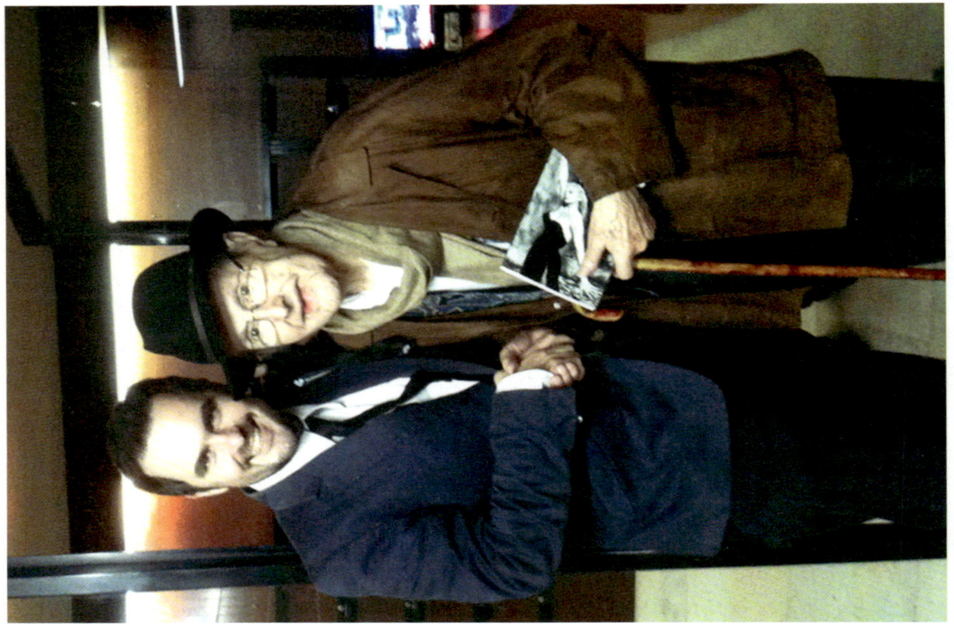

D 4

# 58. DEL TORO, Benicio

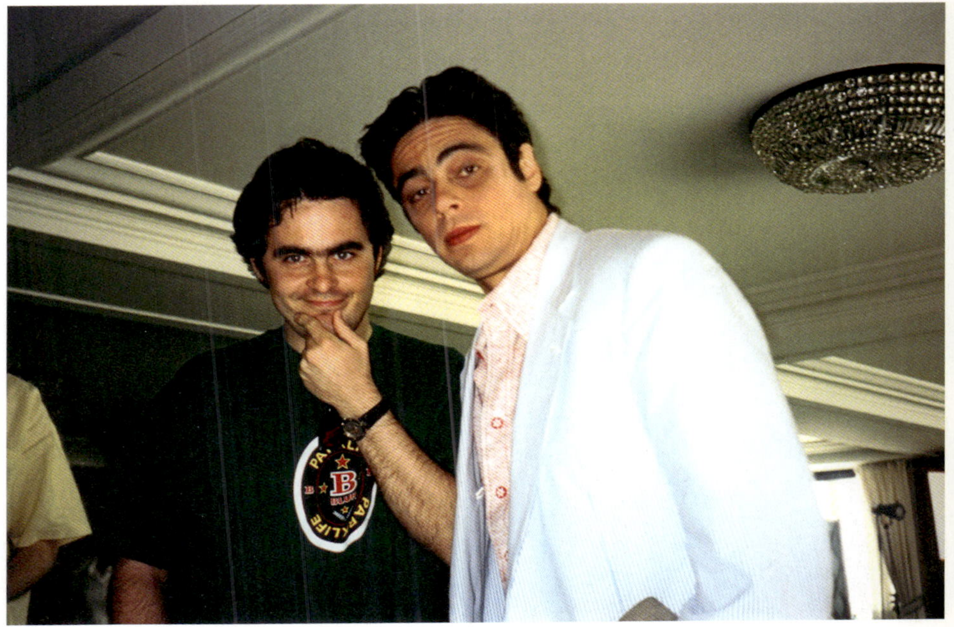

D 5

# 59. DEL TORO, Guillermo

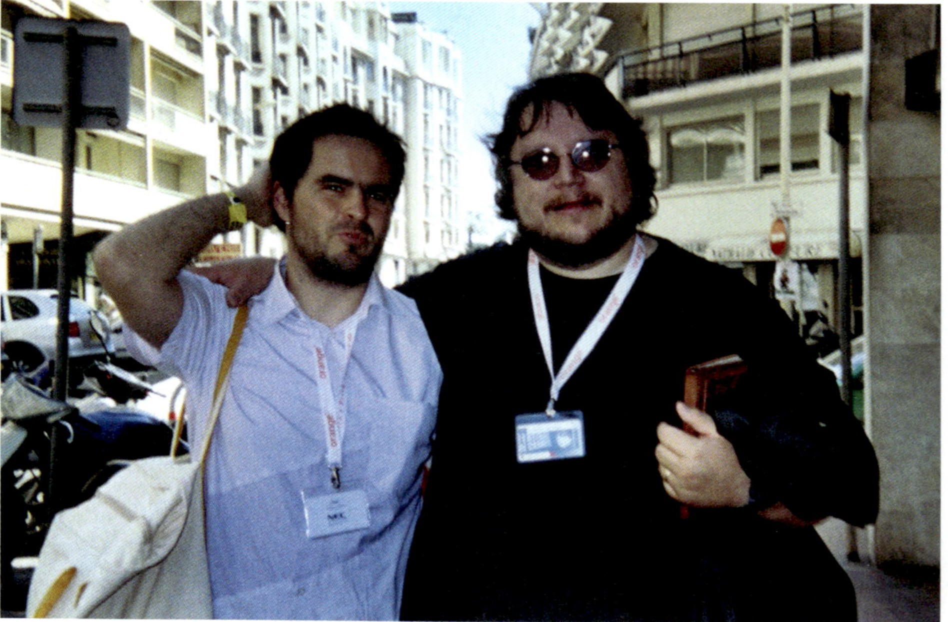

**D 6**

# 60. DEPARDIEU, Guillaume

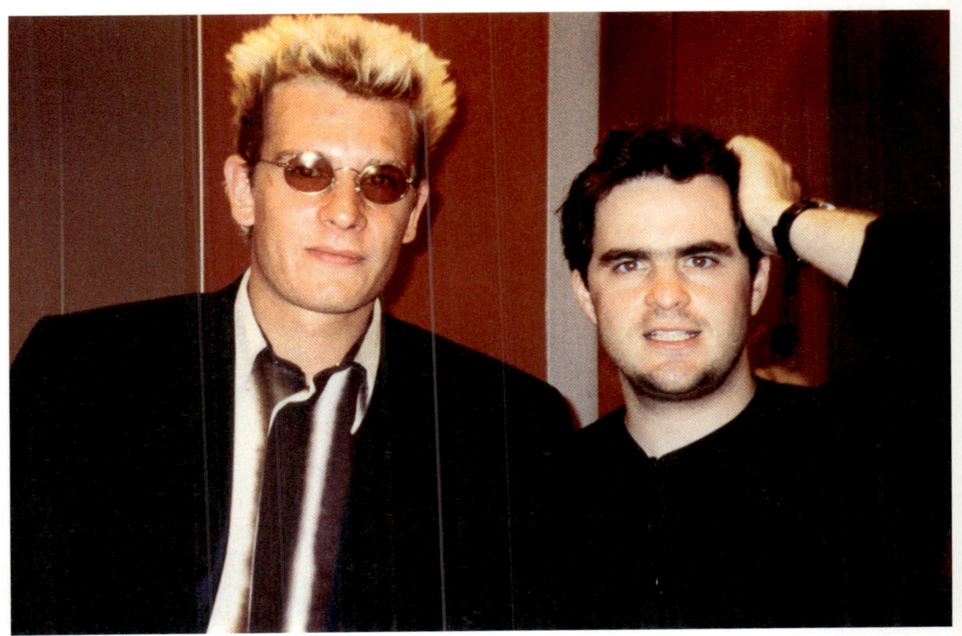

D 7

# 61. DEPP, Johnny

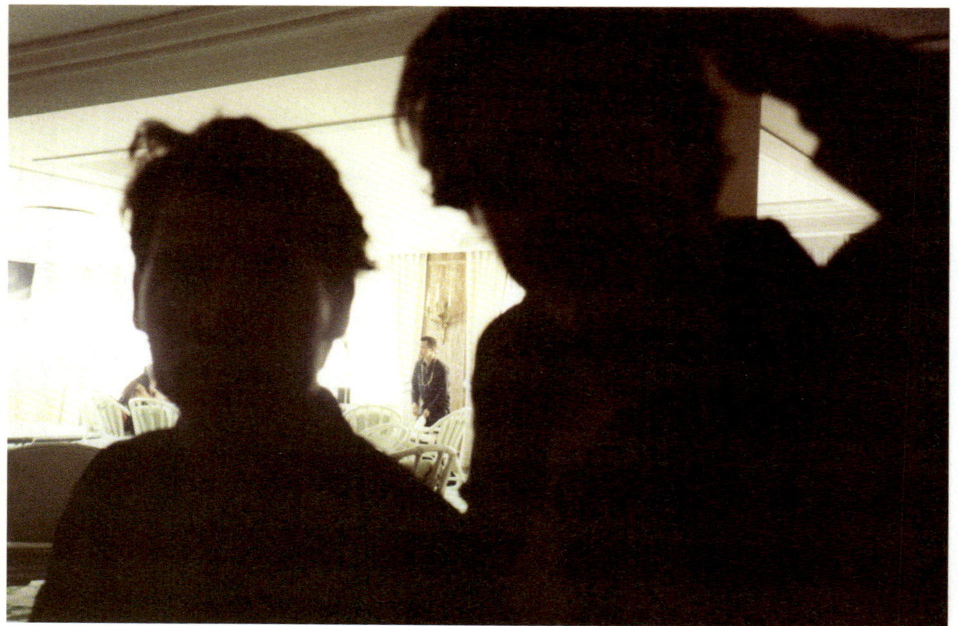

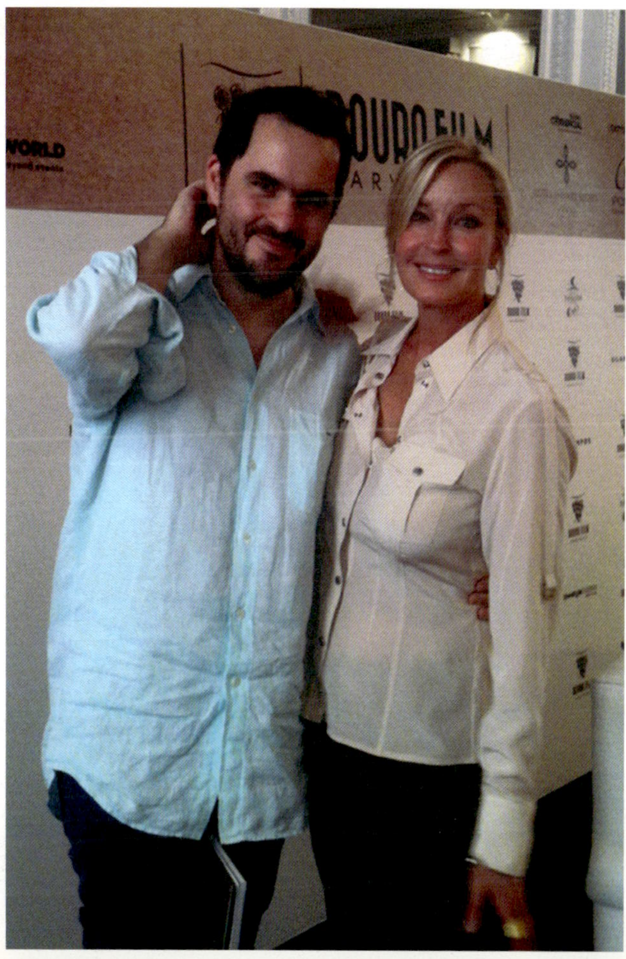

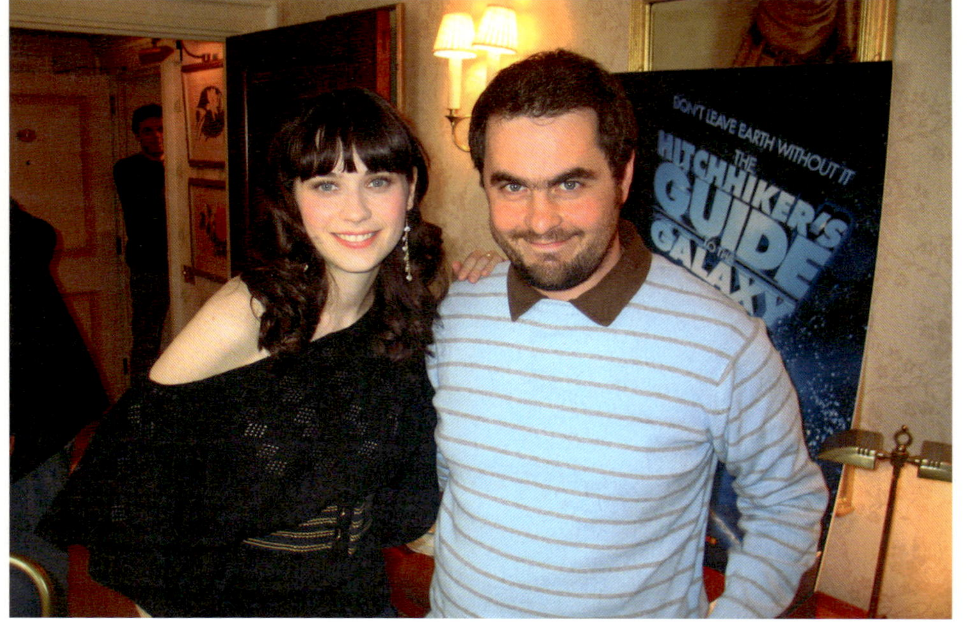
DON'T LEAVE EARTH WITHOUT IT
THE
HITCHHIKER'S
GUIDE
TO THE
GALAXY

D 10

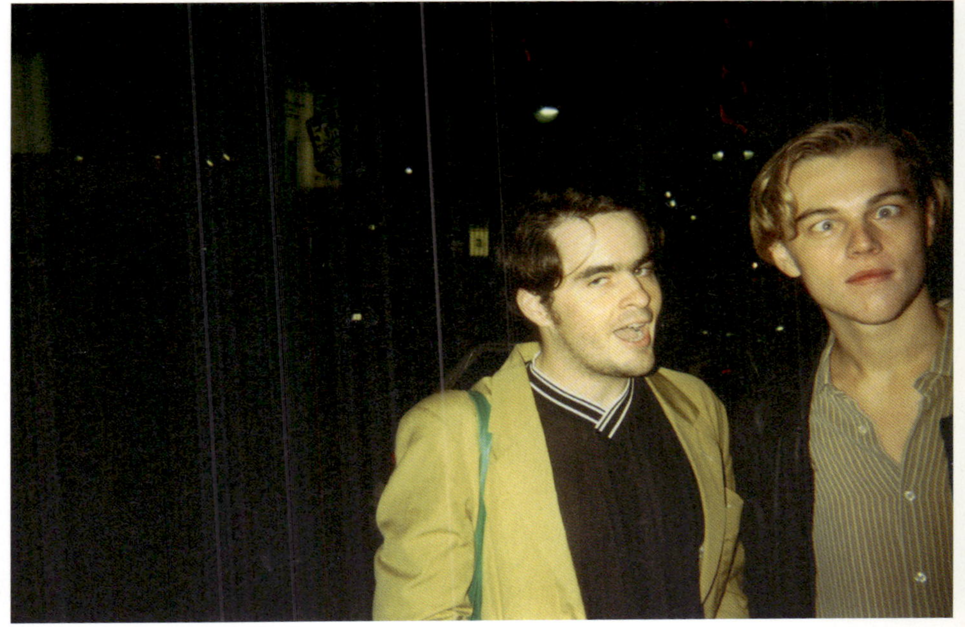

# 65. DILLON, Matt

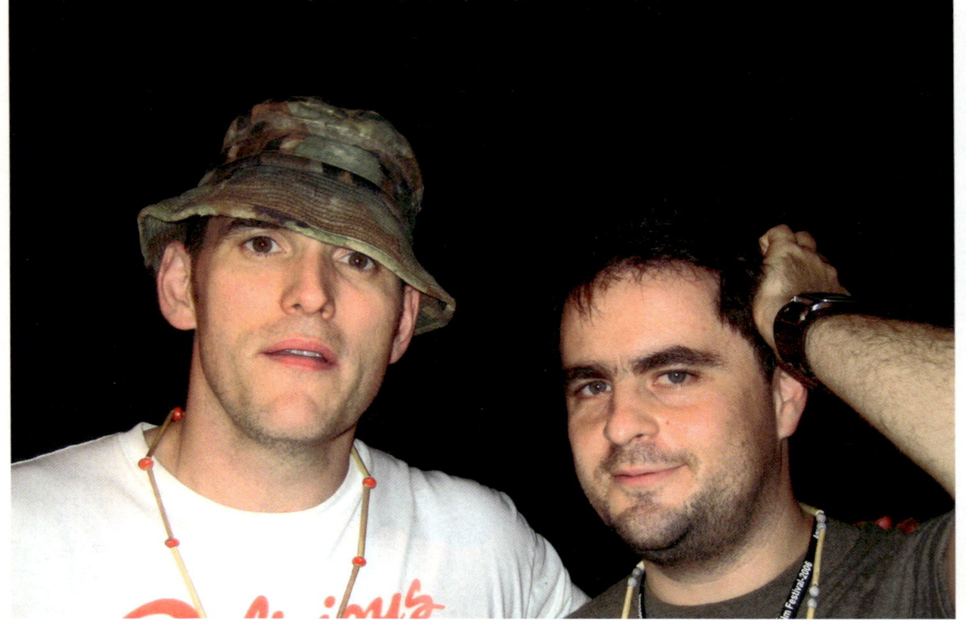

D 12

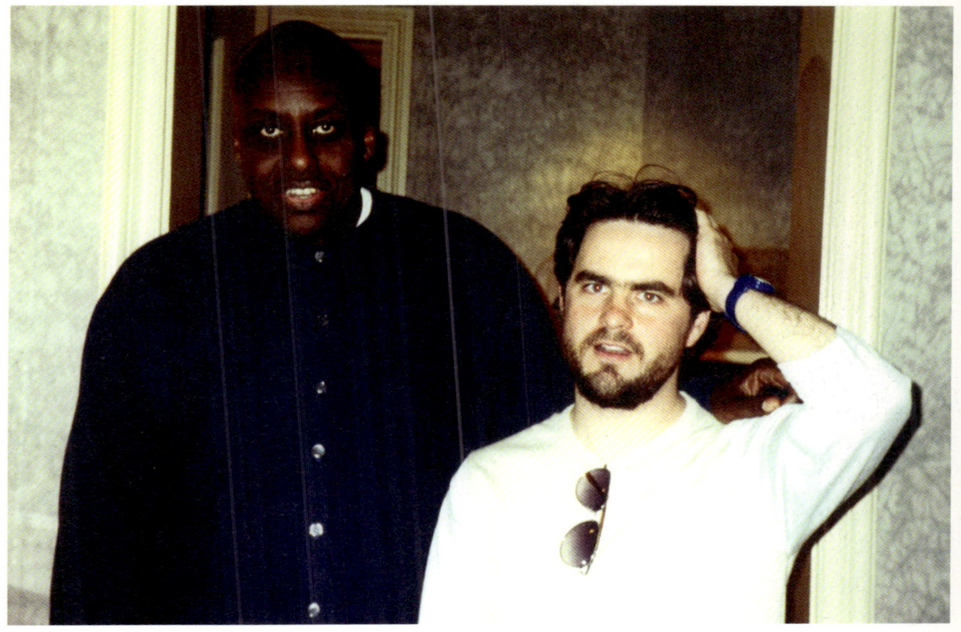

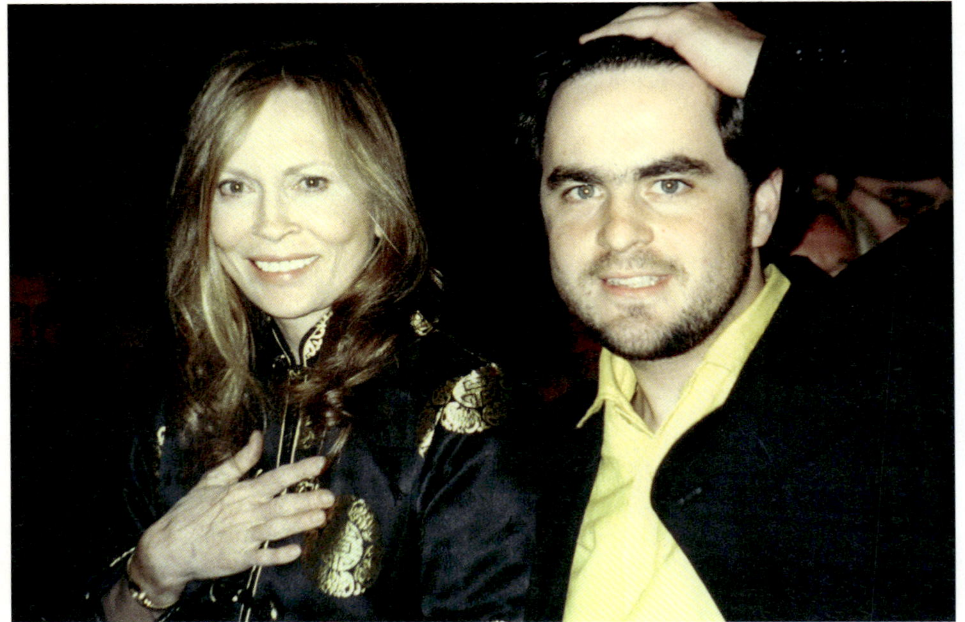

D 14

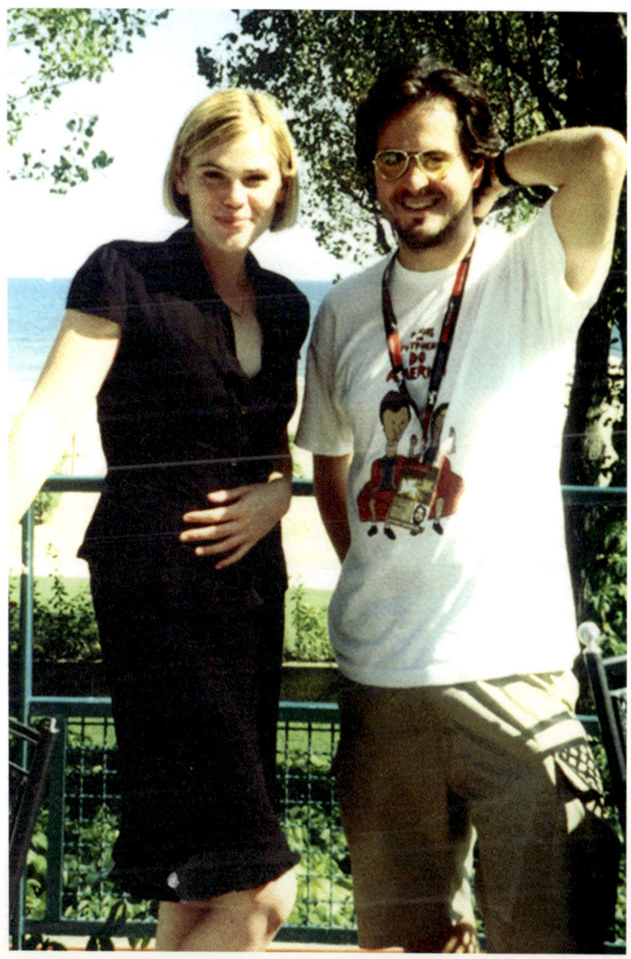

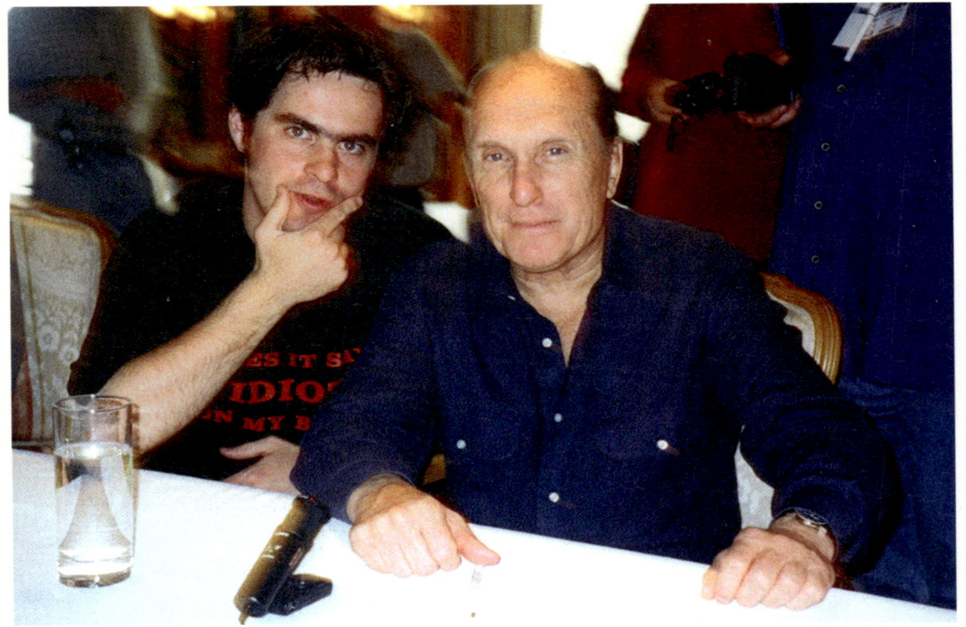


D 16

# 70. EFRON, Zac / 71. BLEU, Corbin

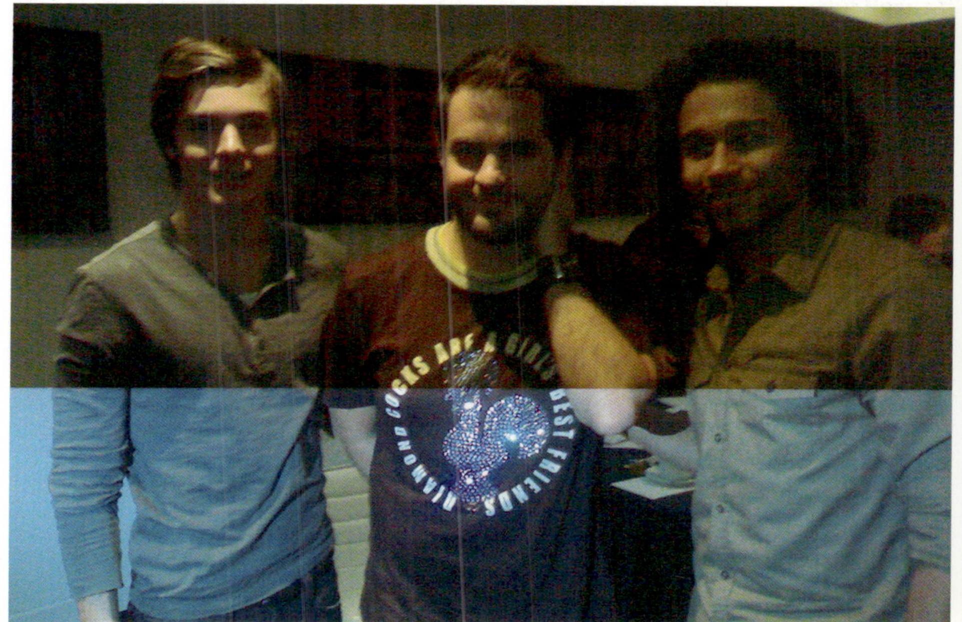

E 1

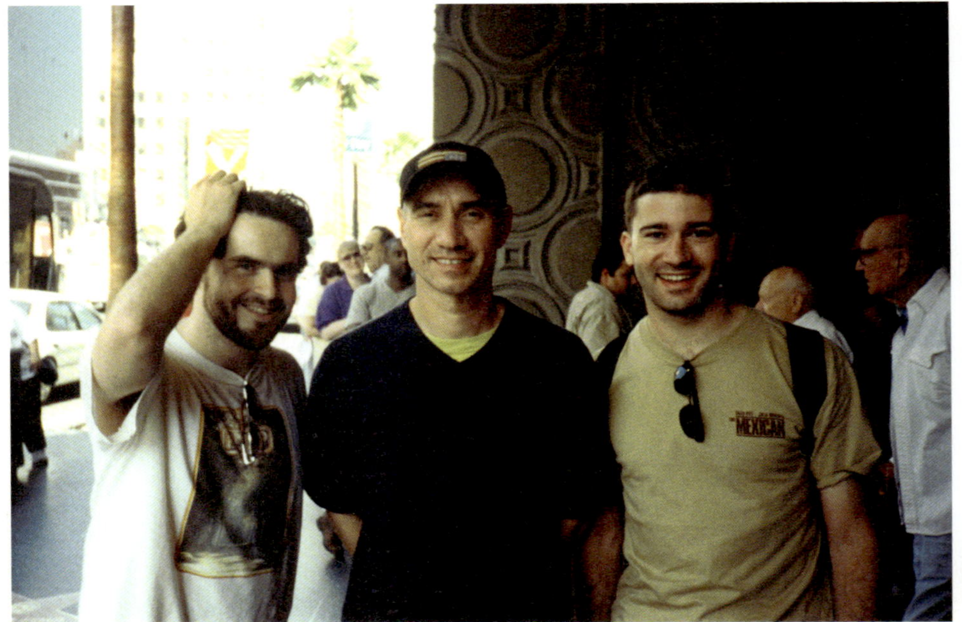

# 74. FARÈS, Nadia

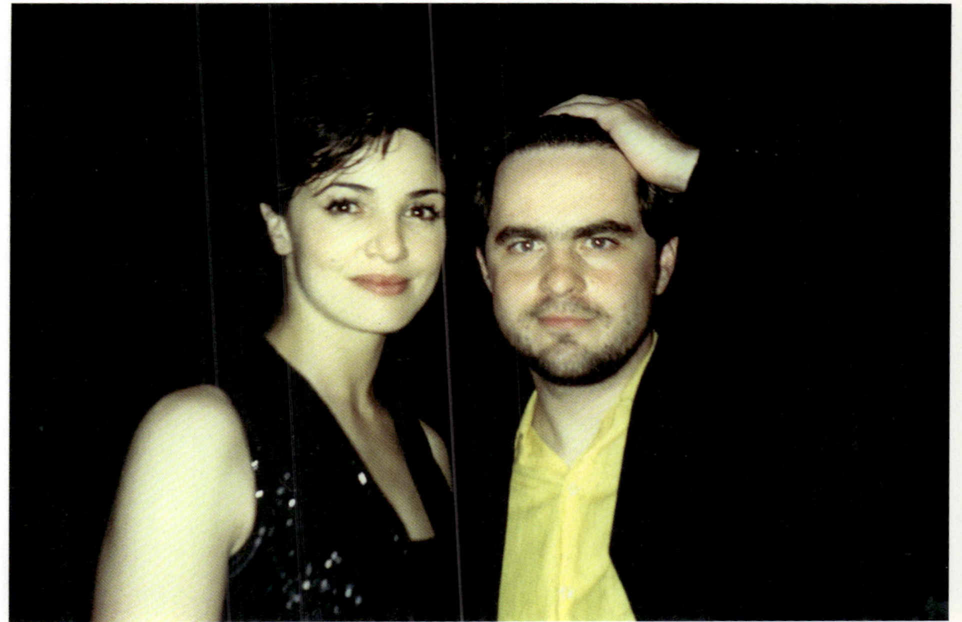

F 1

# 75. FONDA, Bridget

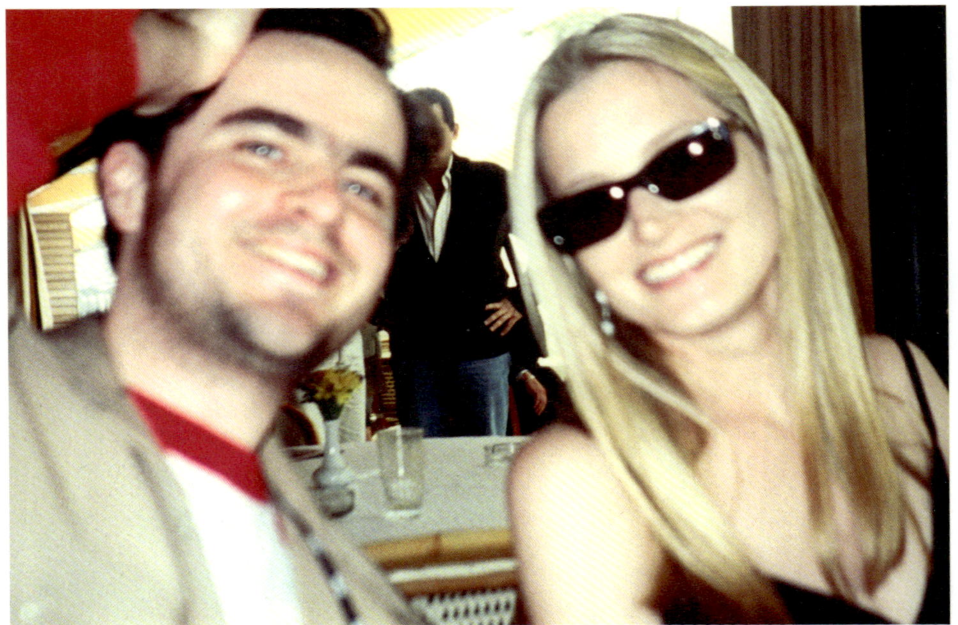

F 2

# 76. FOX, Kerry

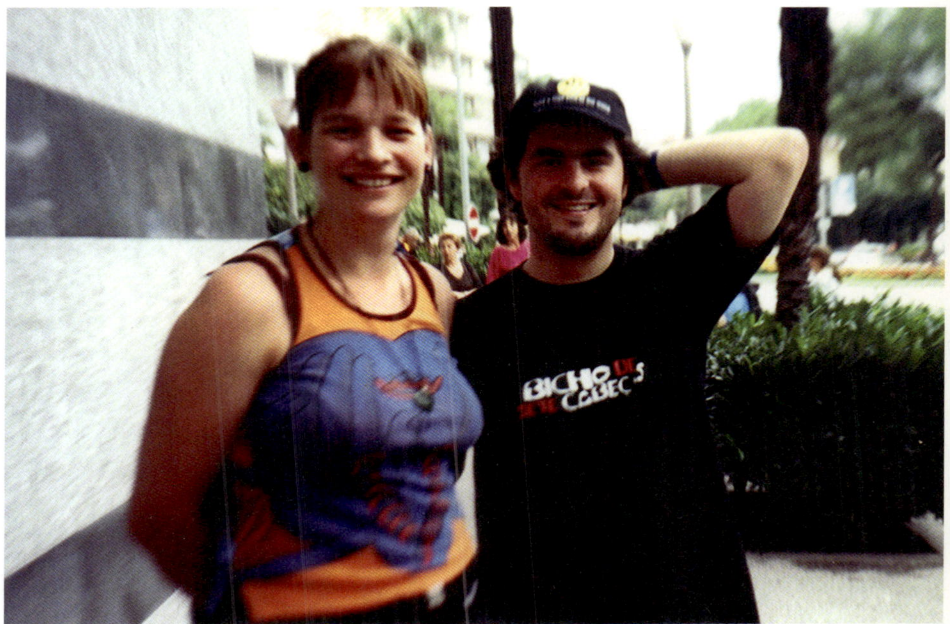

# 77. FRANCO, James

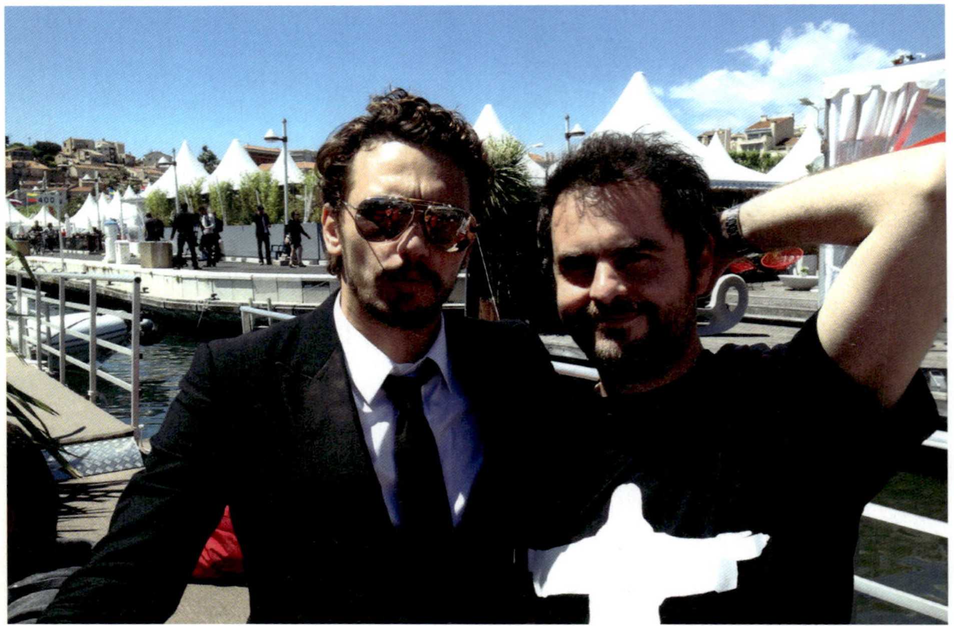

F 4

# 78. GALLO, Vincent

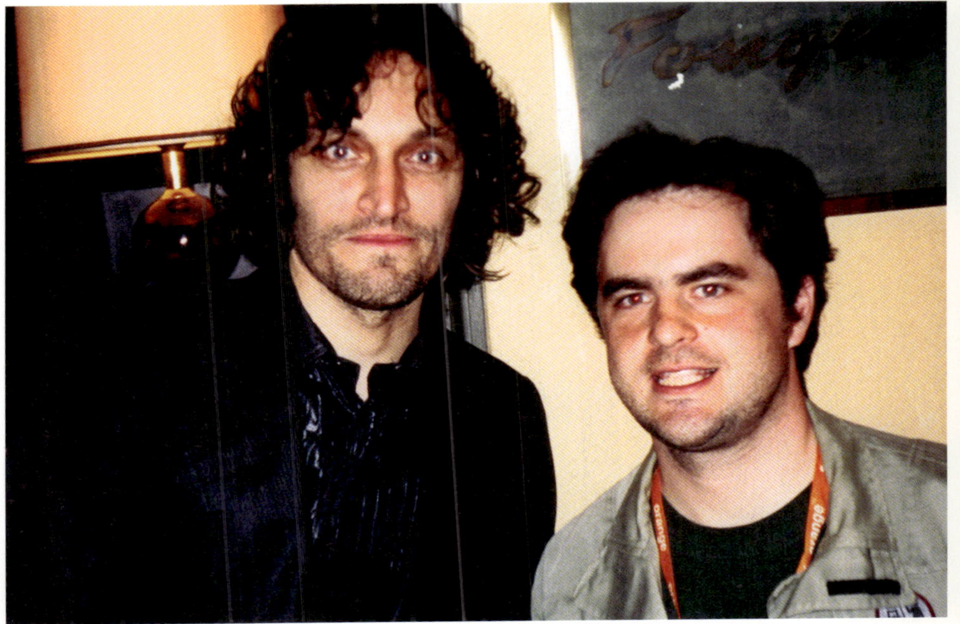

# 79. GARCÍA BERNAL, Gael

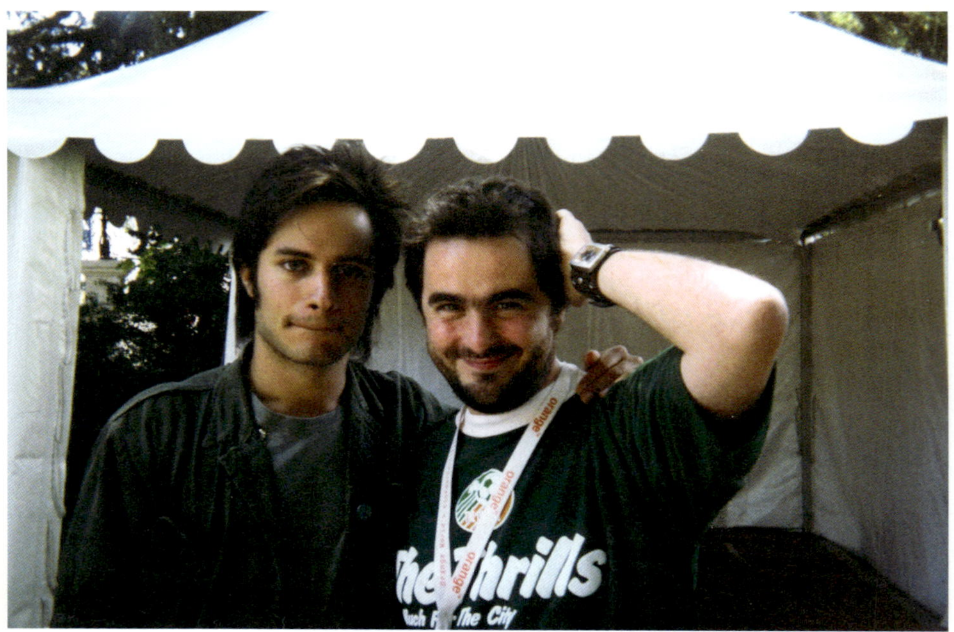

G 2

# 80. GERSHON, Gina

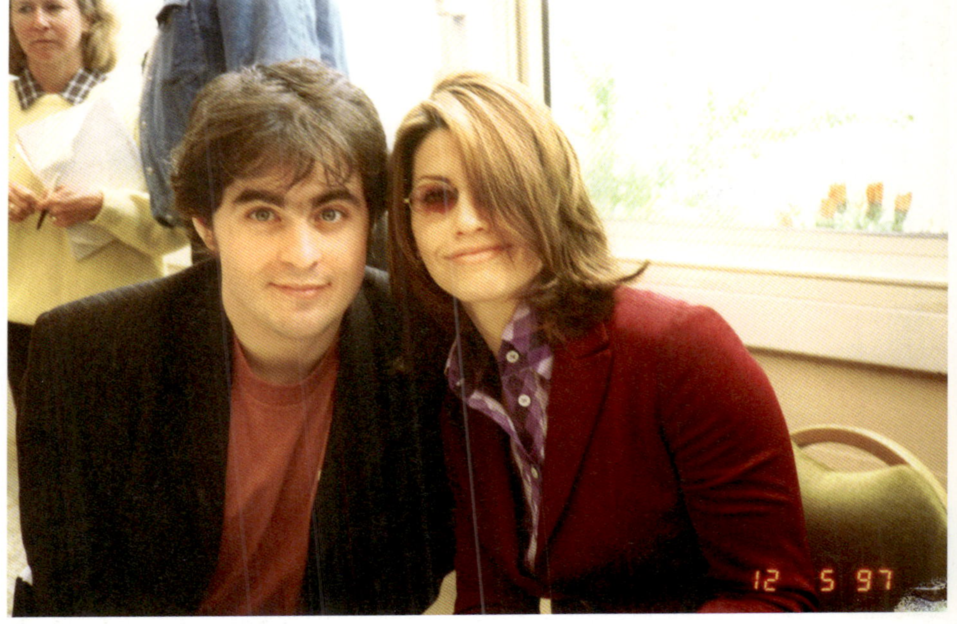



G 3

# 81. GILAIN, Marie

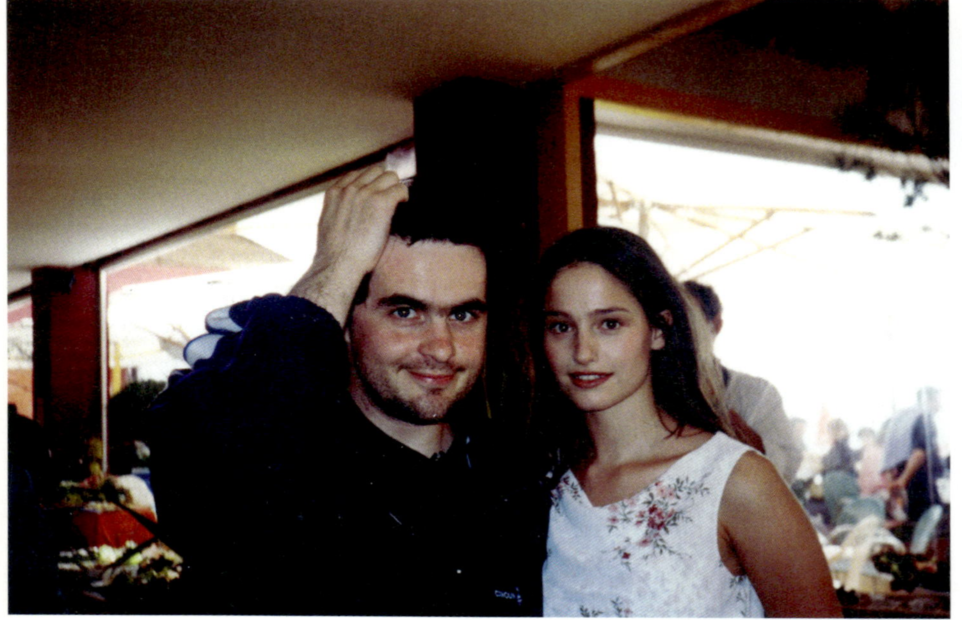

G 4

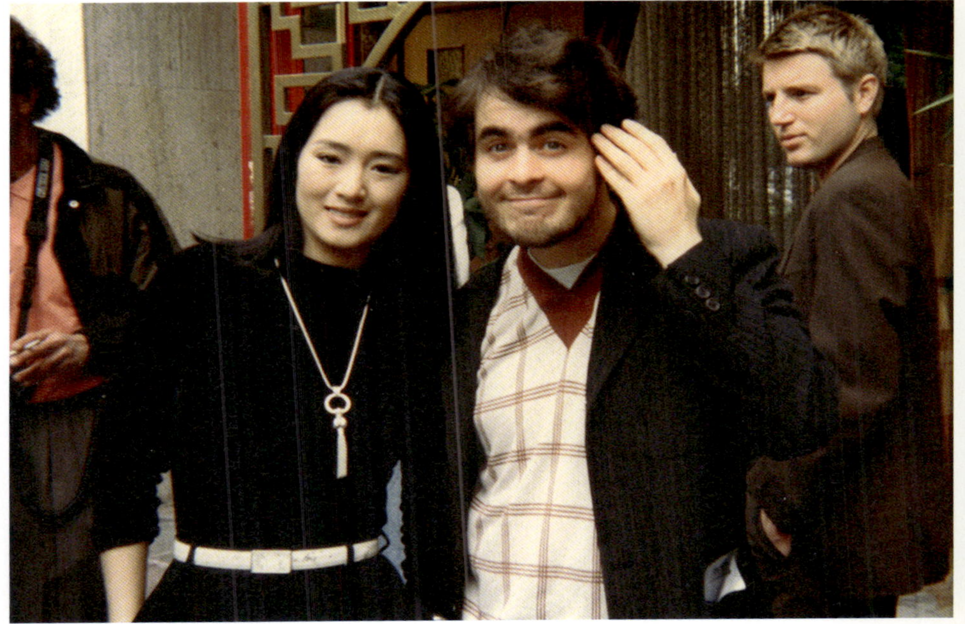

# 83. GOSLING, Ryan

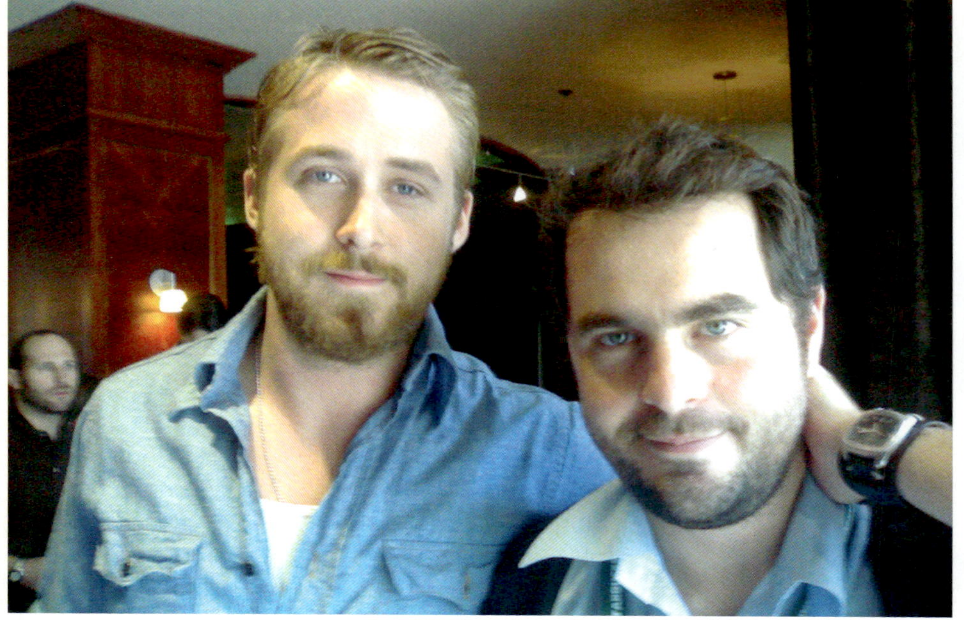

G 6

# 84. GRAHAM, Heather

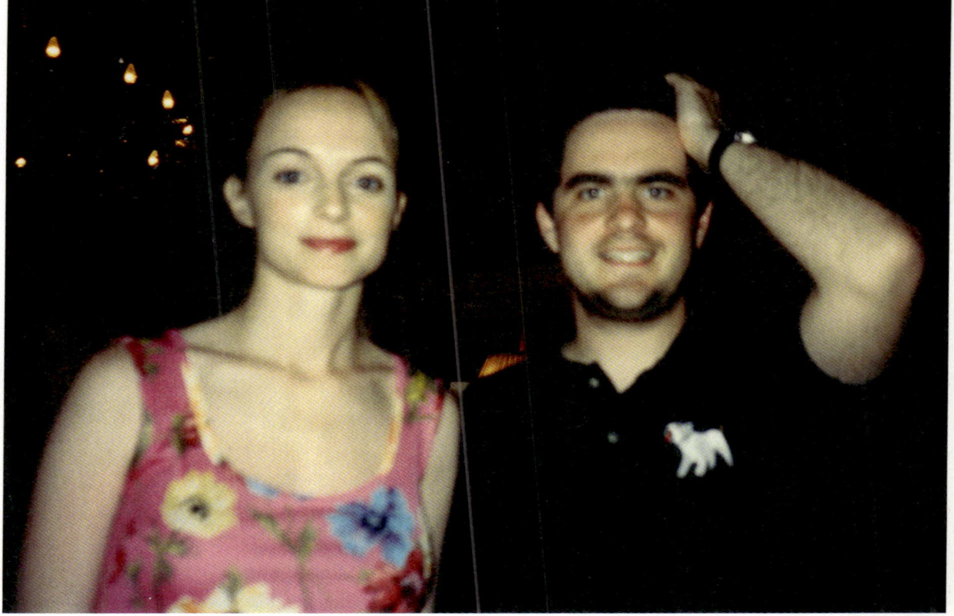

G 7

# 85. GREEN, Eva

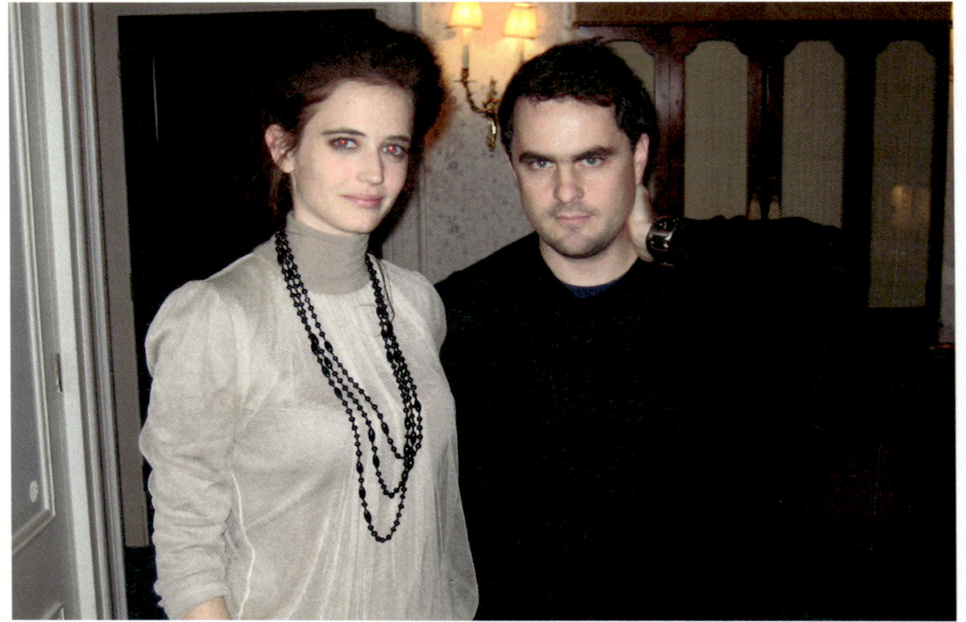

G 8

# 86. GREY, Sasha

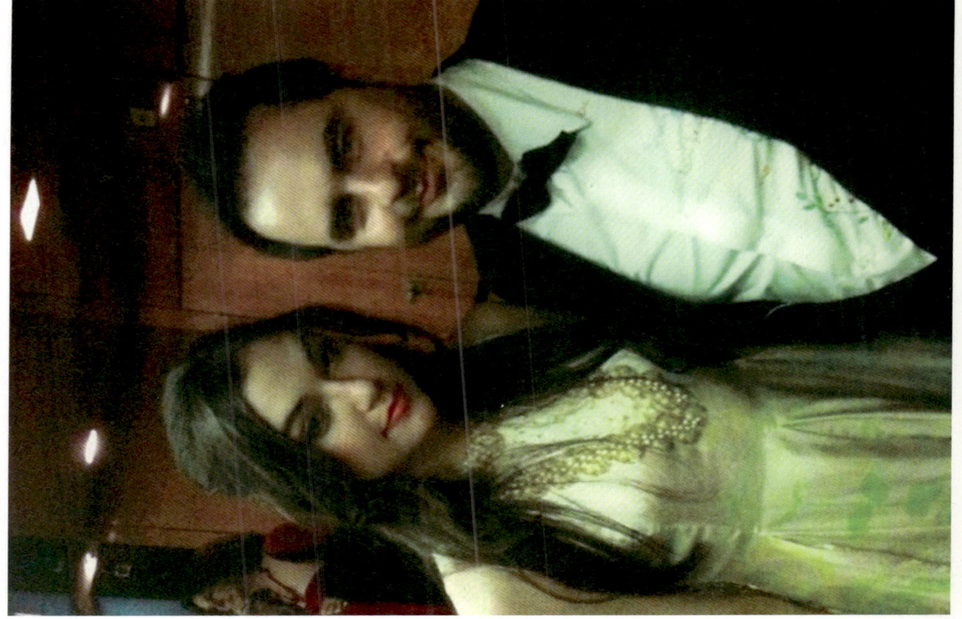

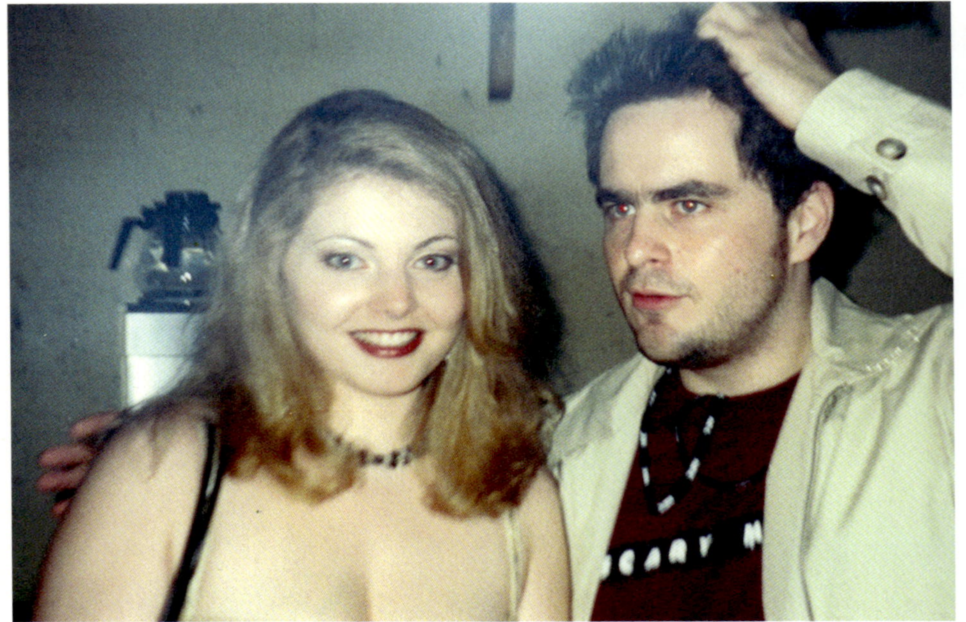

G 10

# 88. HARRIS, Ed

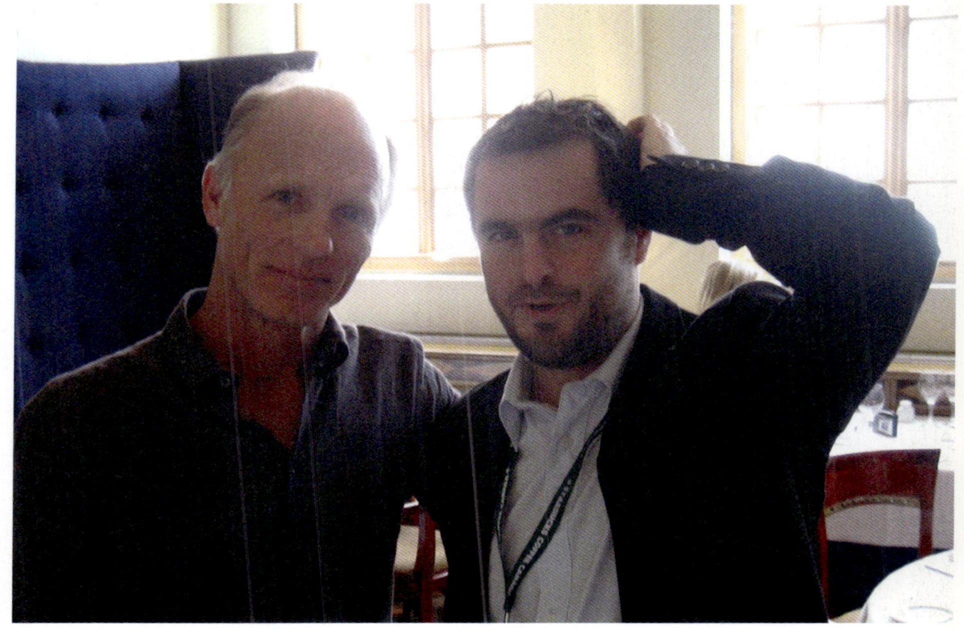

H 1

# 89. HART, Ian

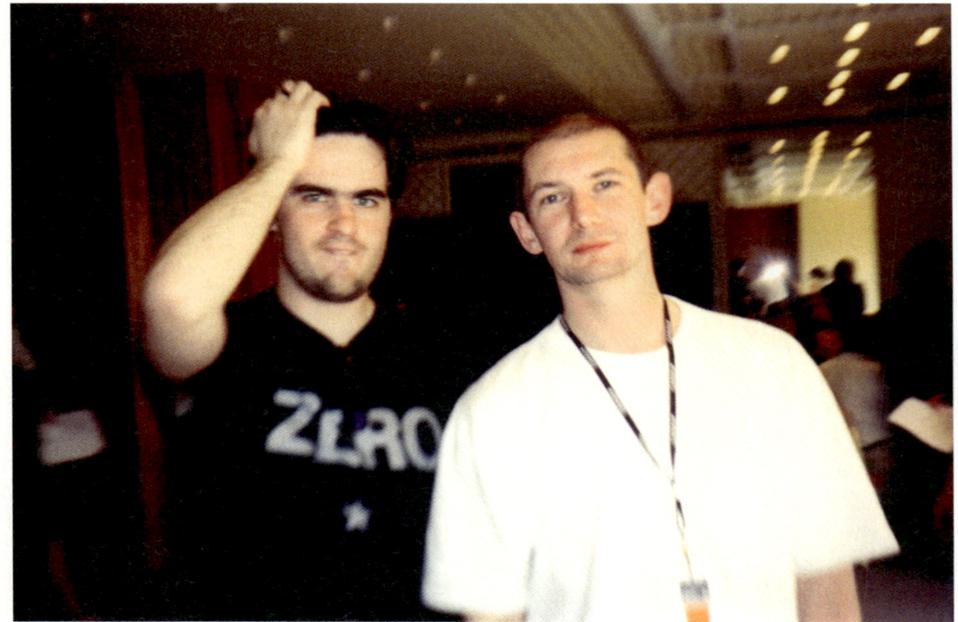

H 2

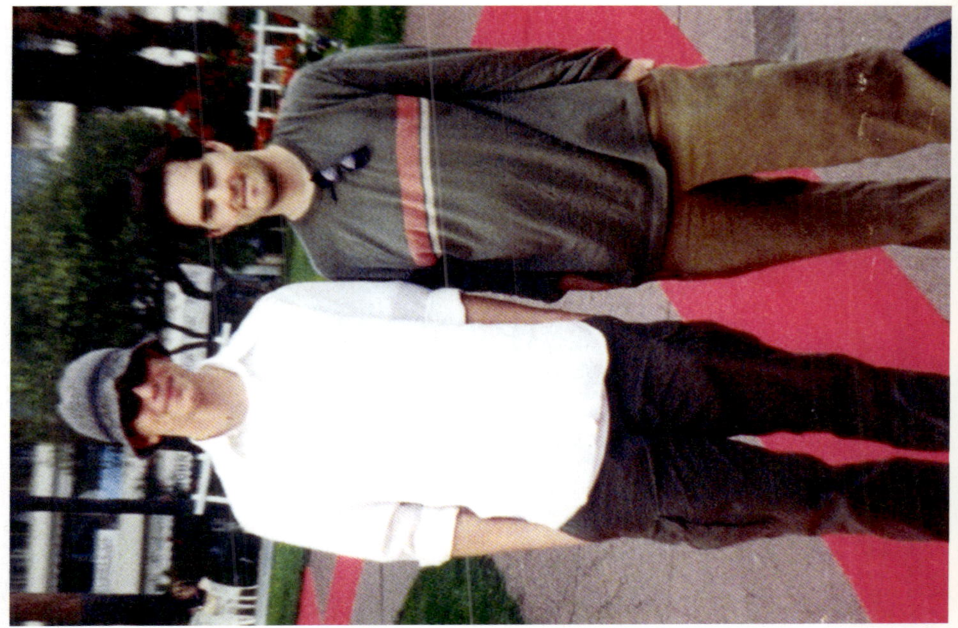

H 3

# 91. HAYEK, Salma

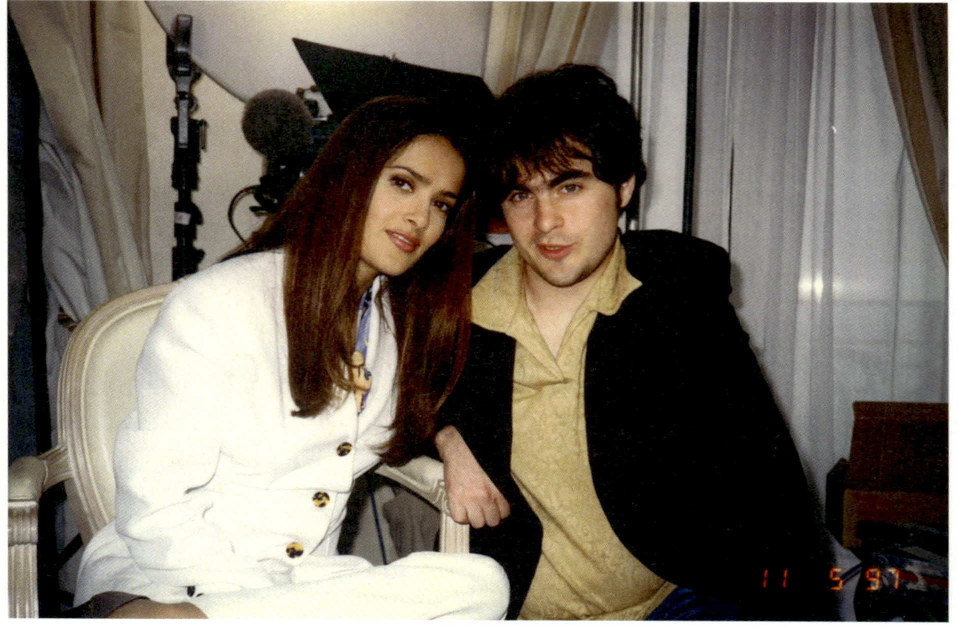

H 4

# 92. HIRSCH, Emile

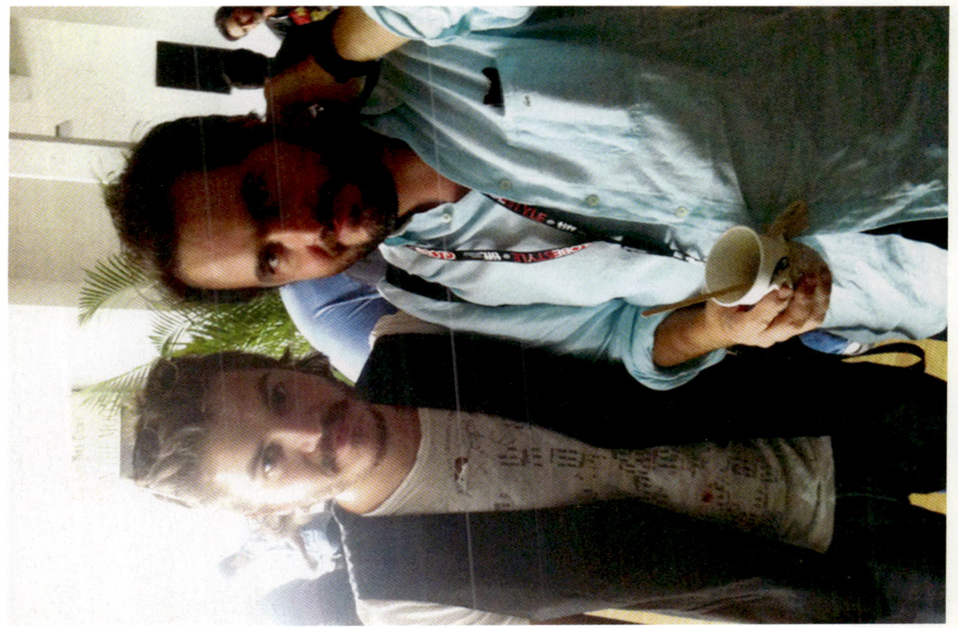

H 5

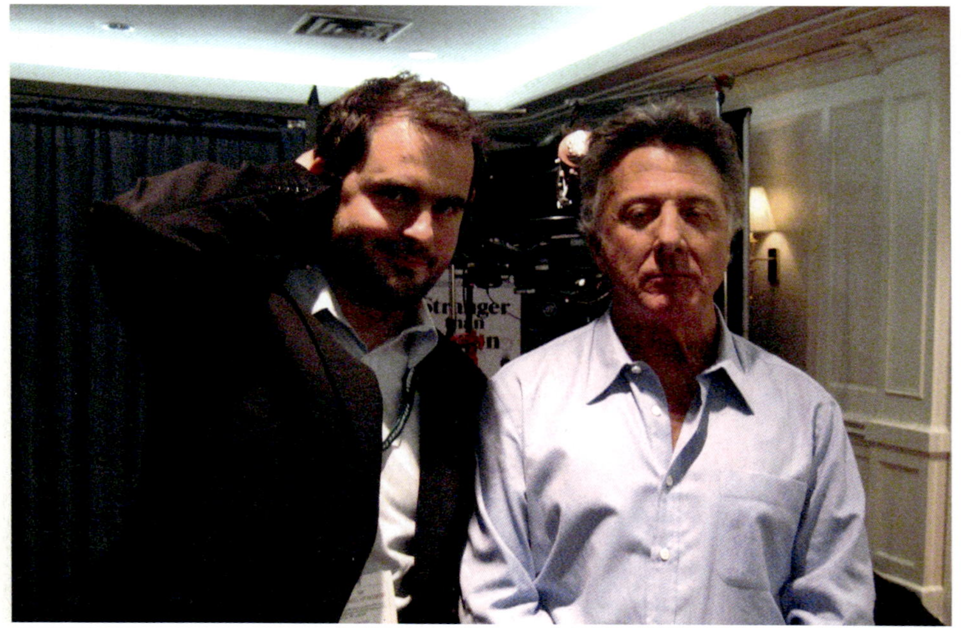
stranger
than
fiction

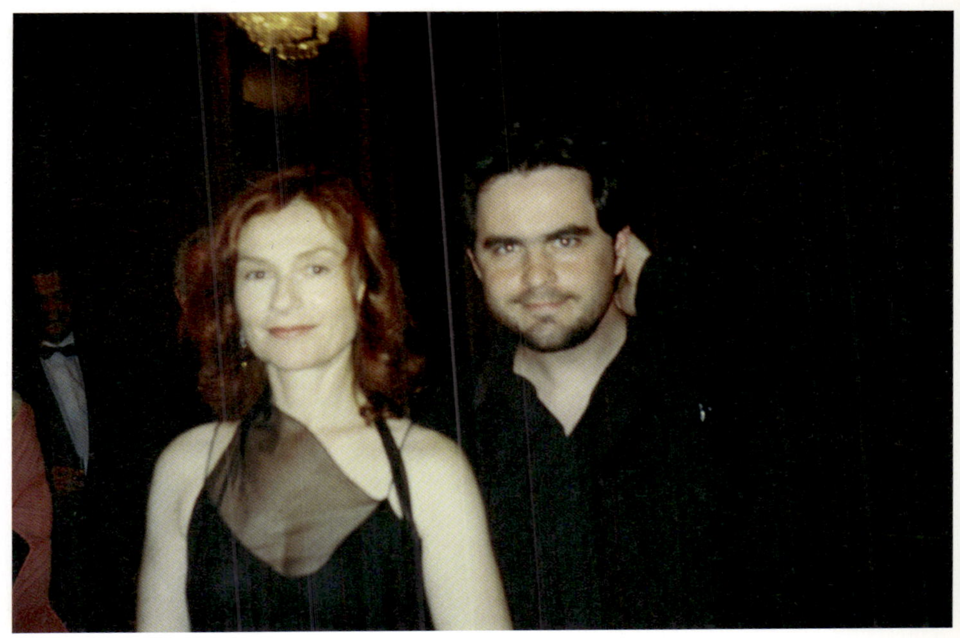

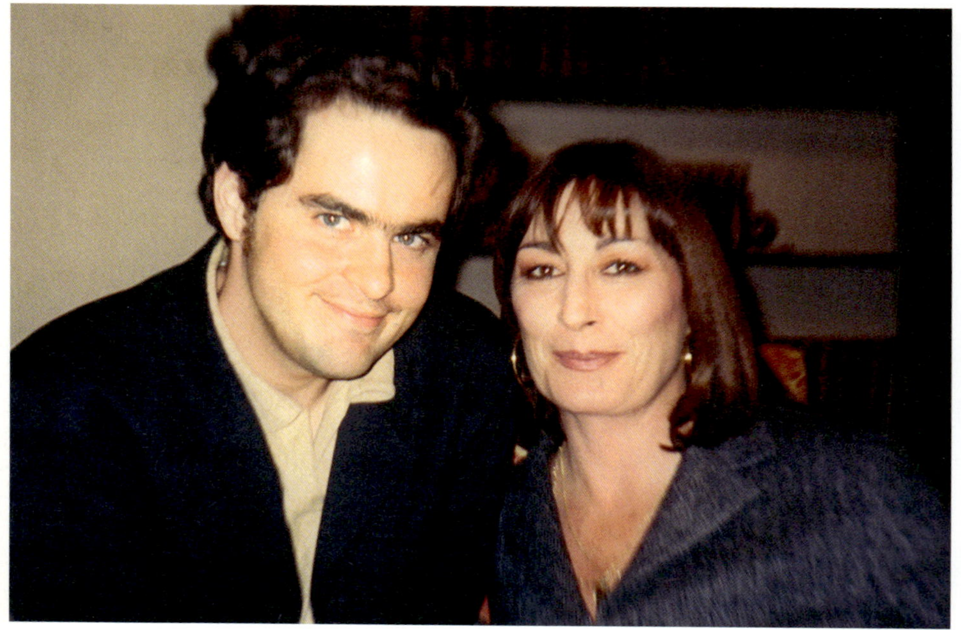

H 8

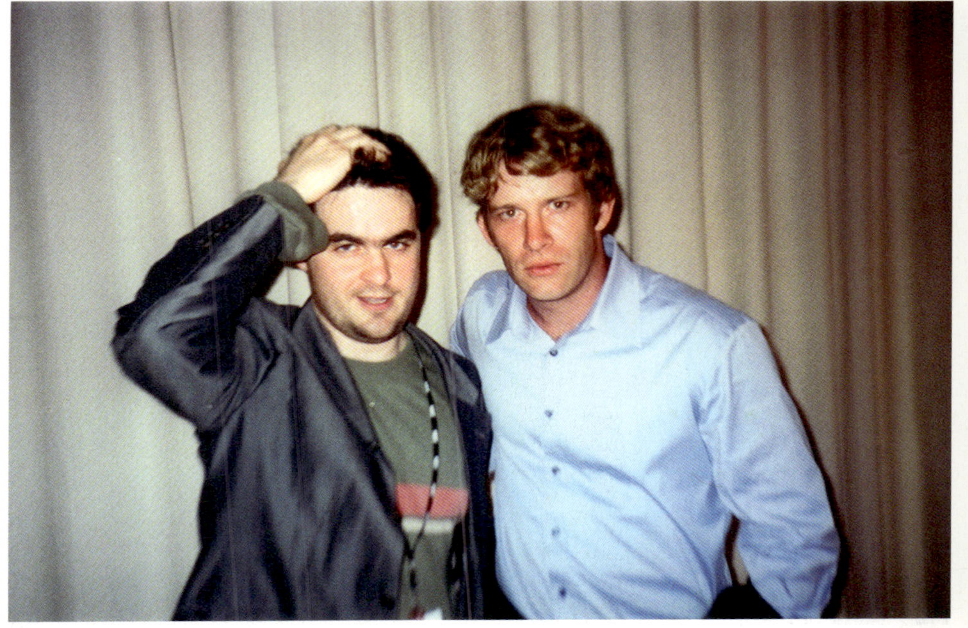

J 1

# 97. JOHANSON, Jay-Jay

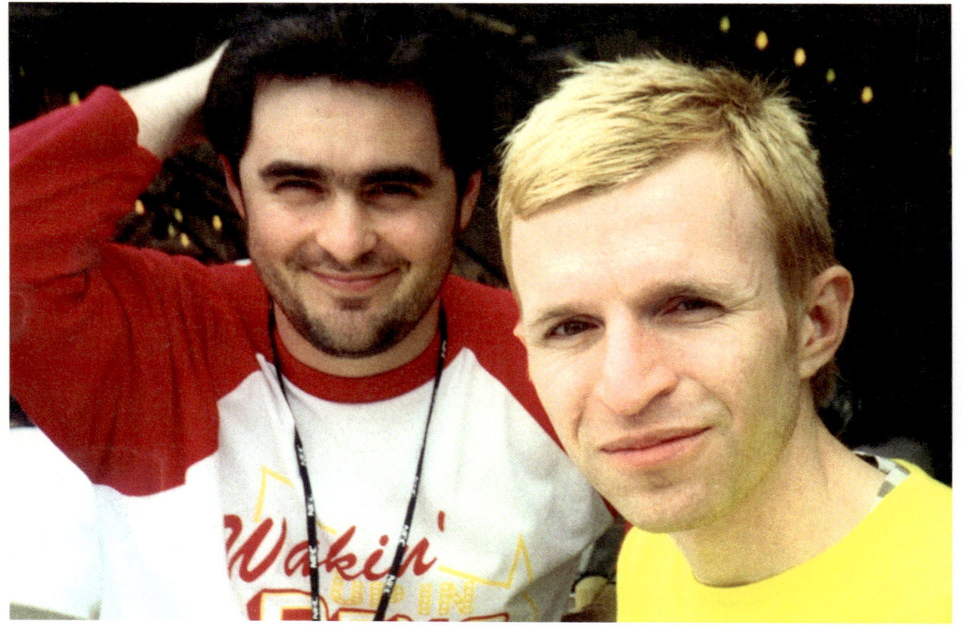

J 2

# 98. JOVOVICH, Milla

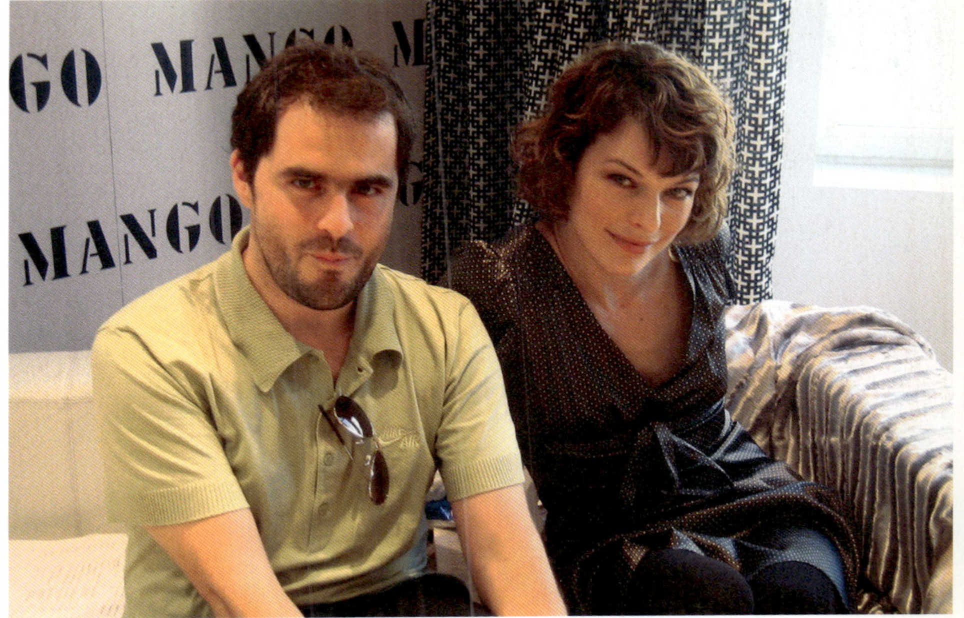


J 3

# 99. KASSOVITZ, Mathieu

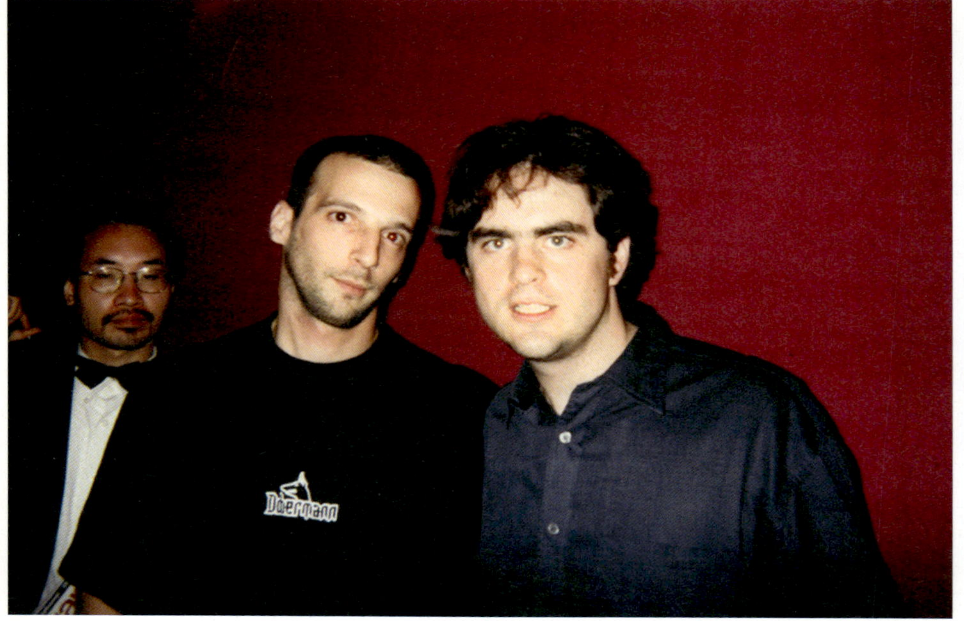

K 1

# 100. KING, Larry

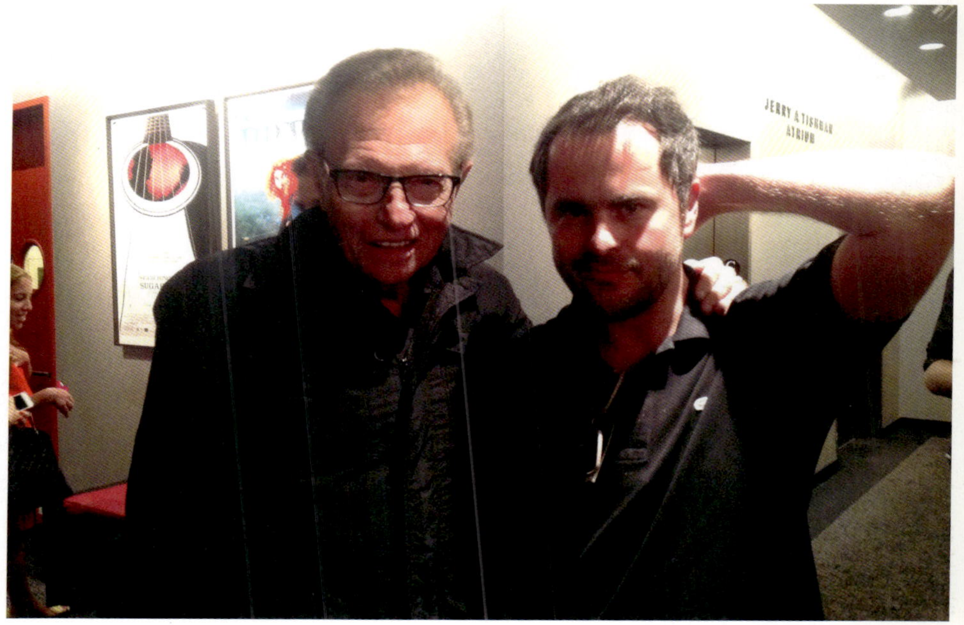


K 2

# 101. KRUGER, Diane

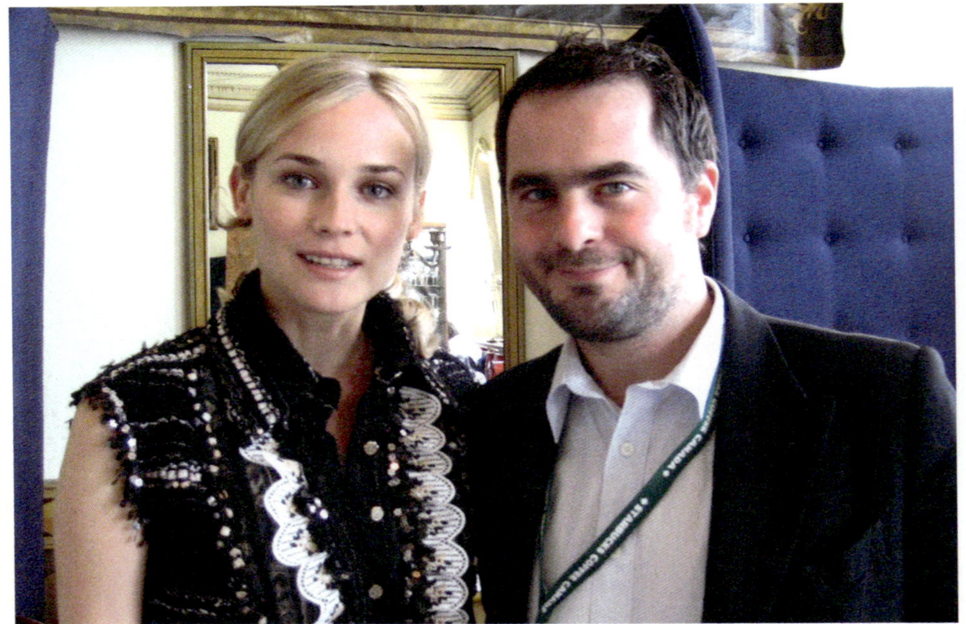

K 3

# 102. KUSTURICA, Emir

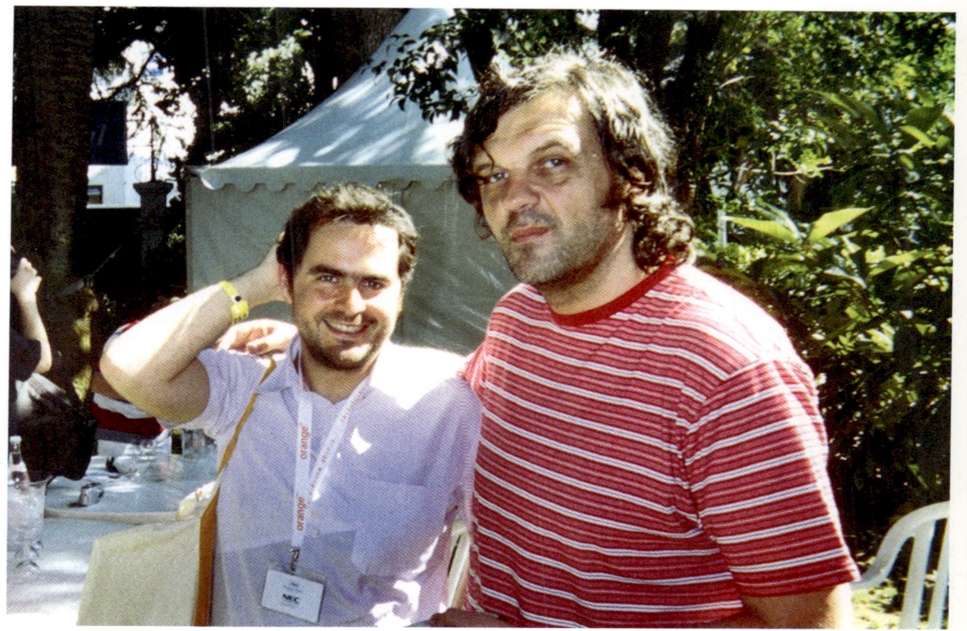

K 4

# 103. LAMBERT, Wilson

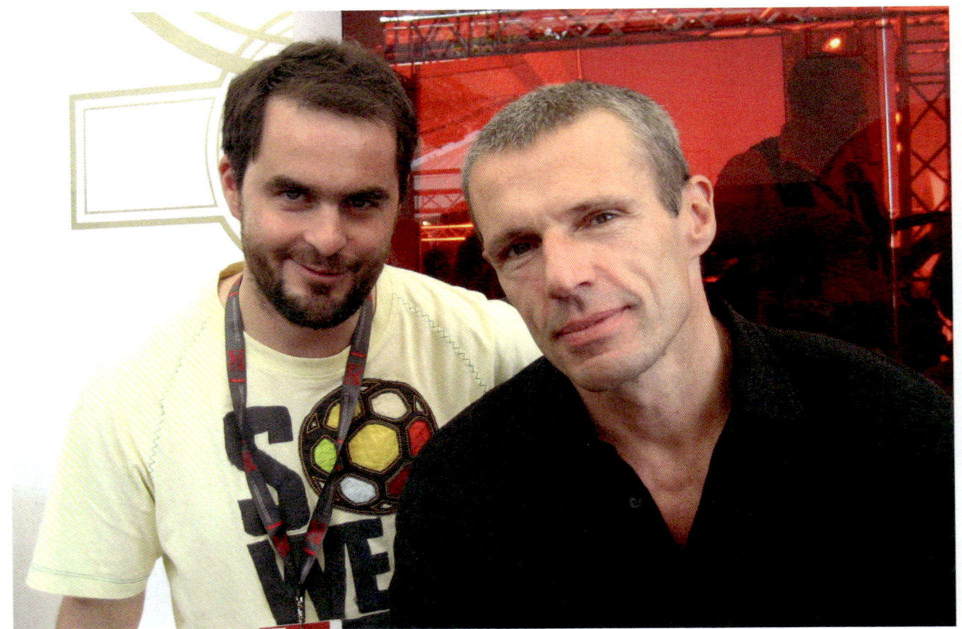

L 1

# 104. LANDAU, Martin

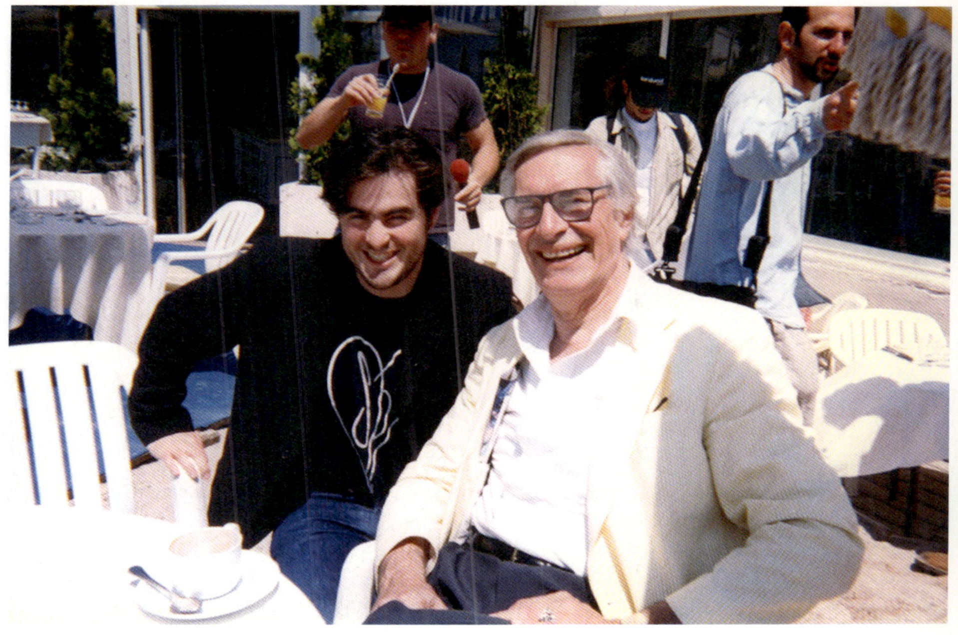

L 2

# 105. LE BESCO, Isabelle

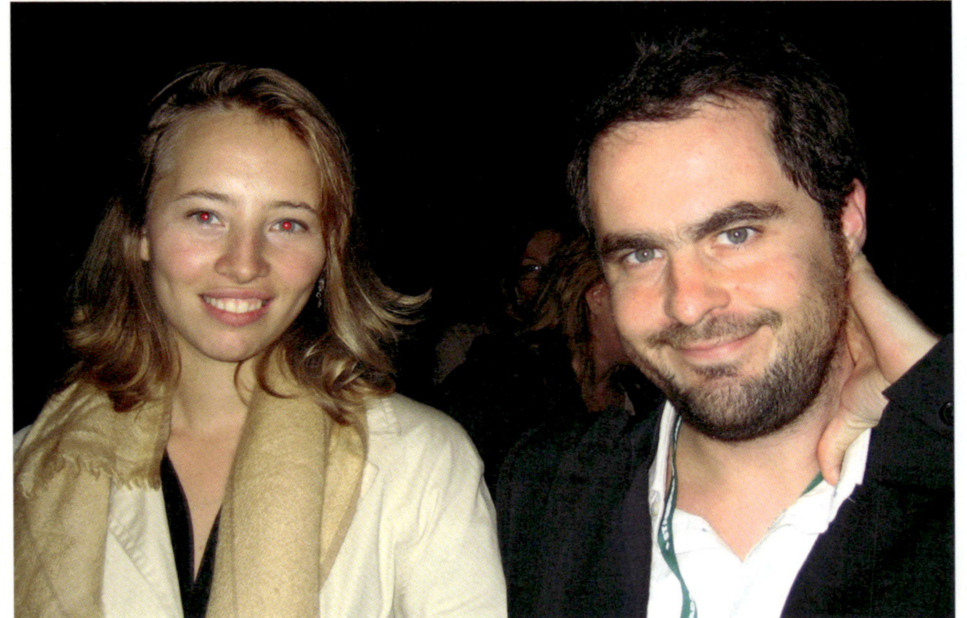

L 3

# 106. LEUNG CHIU WAI, Tony

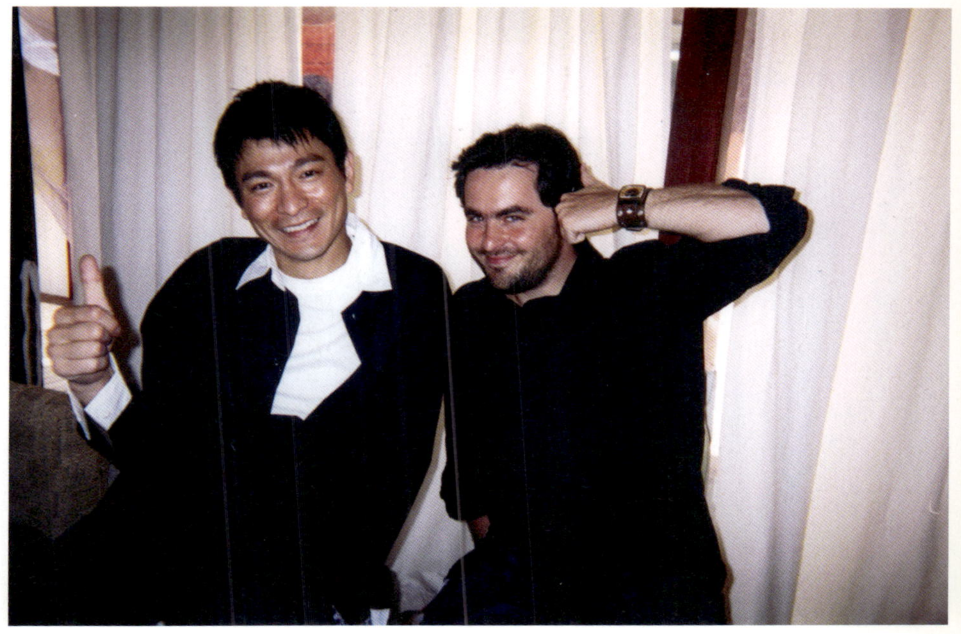

L 4

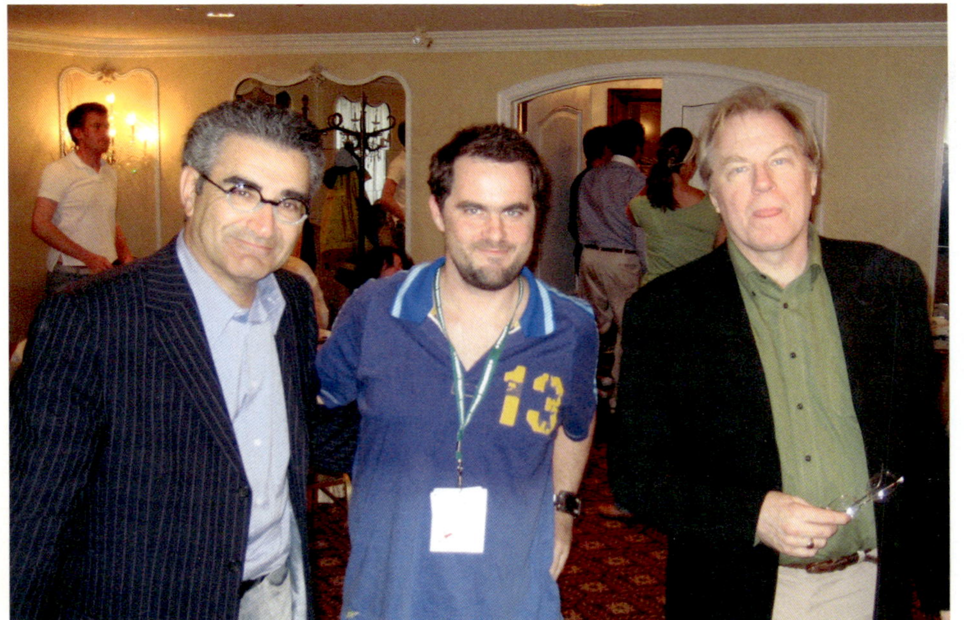

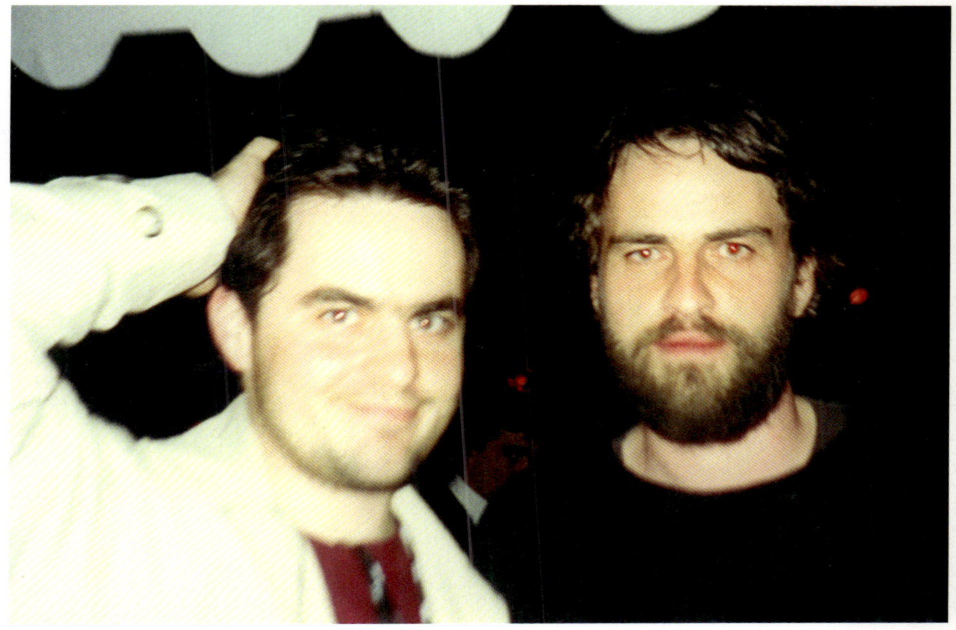

# 110. LYNCH, David

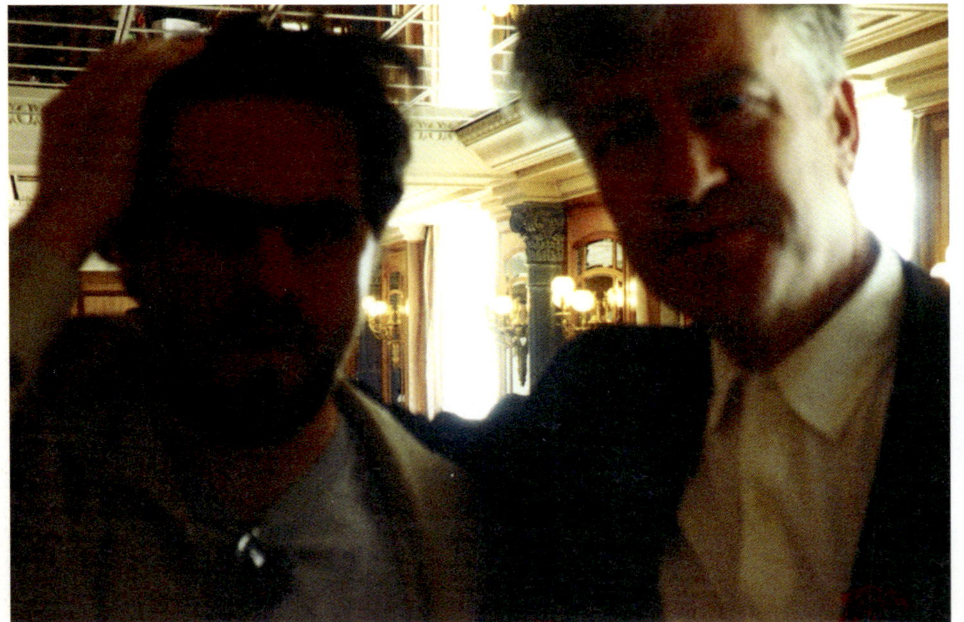

# 111. MACDOWELL, Andie

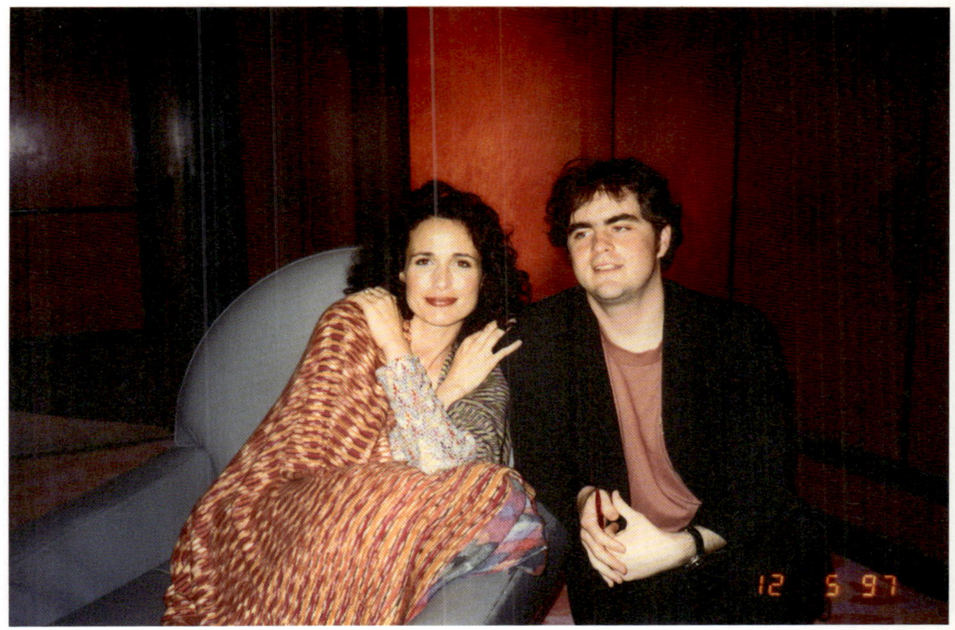



M 1

# 112. MADSEN, Michael

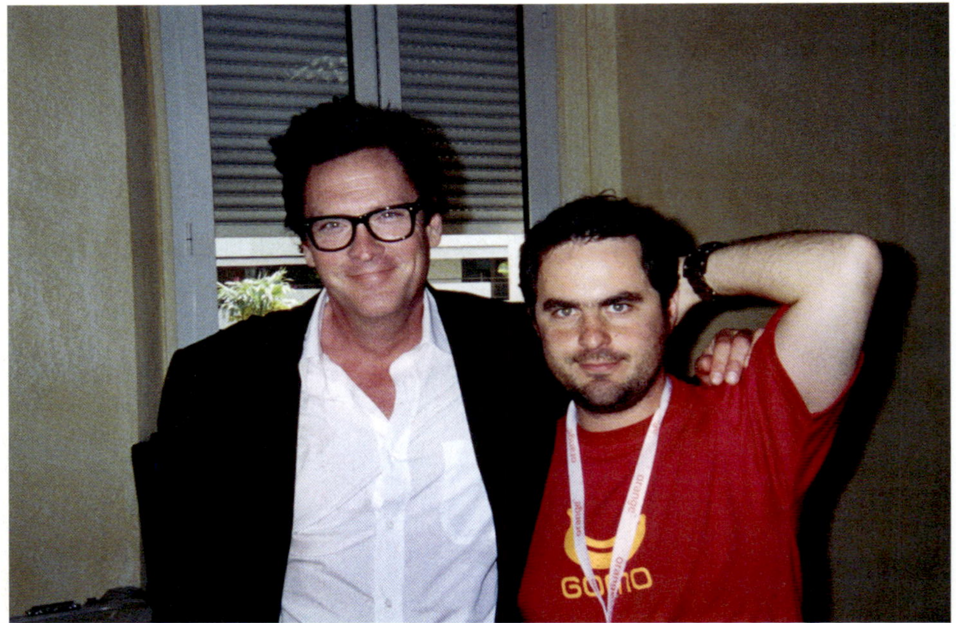

M 2

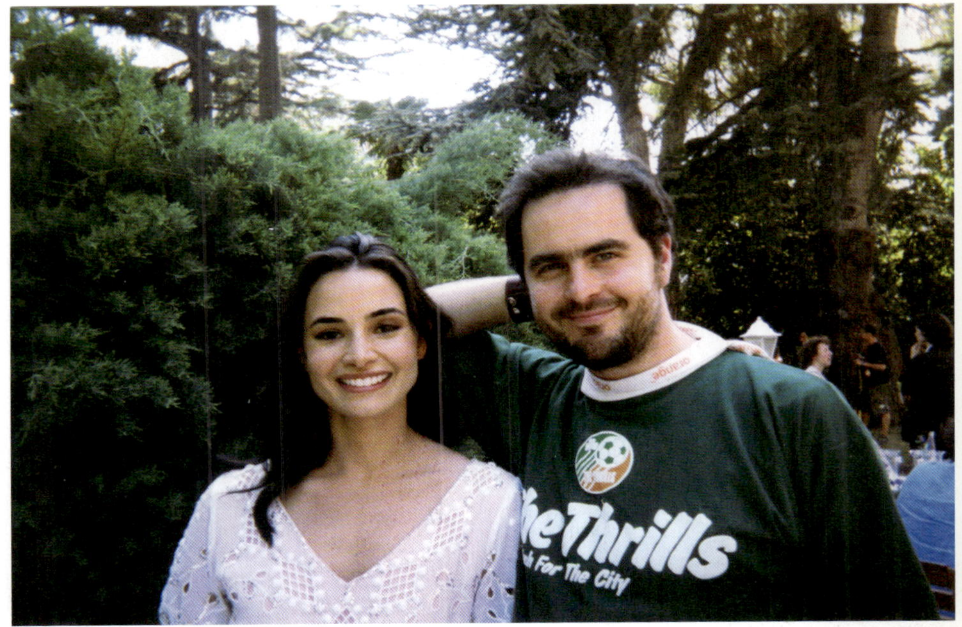
heThrills
For The City

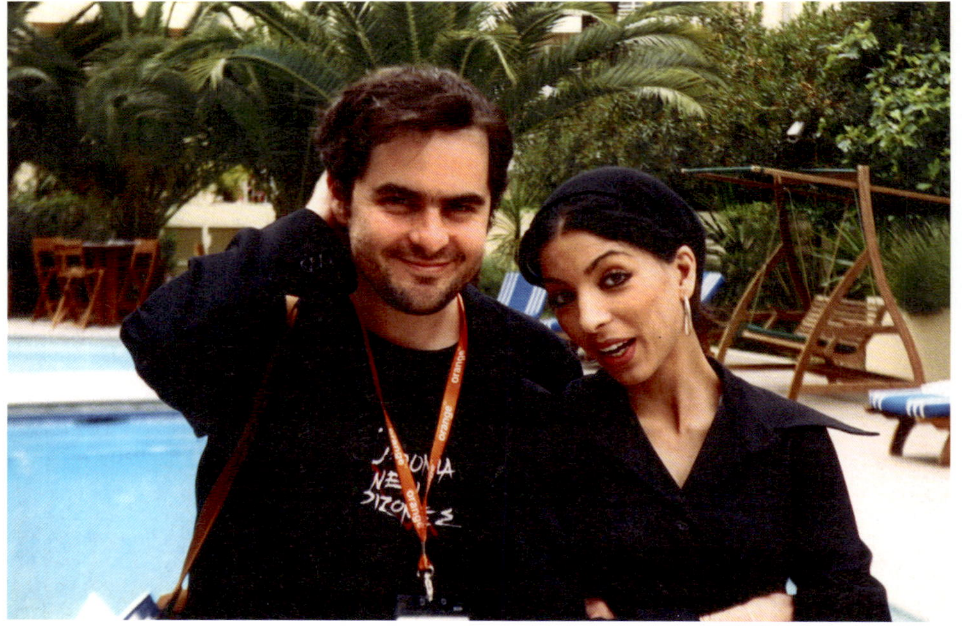

M 4

# 115. MAMET, David

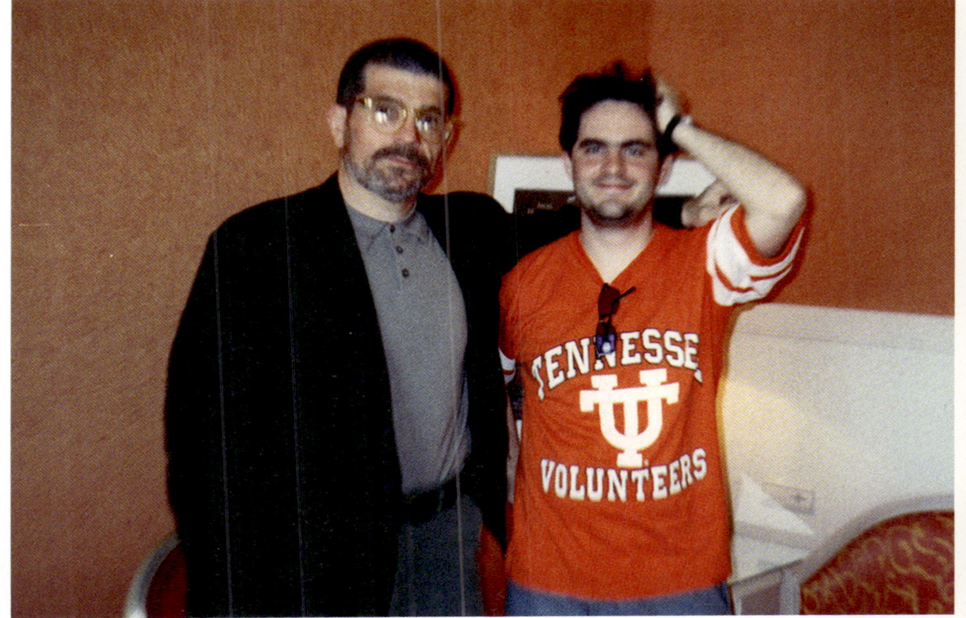


M 5

# 116. McGREGOR, Ewan

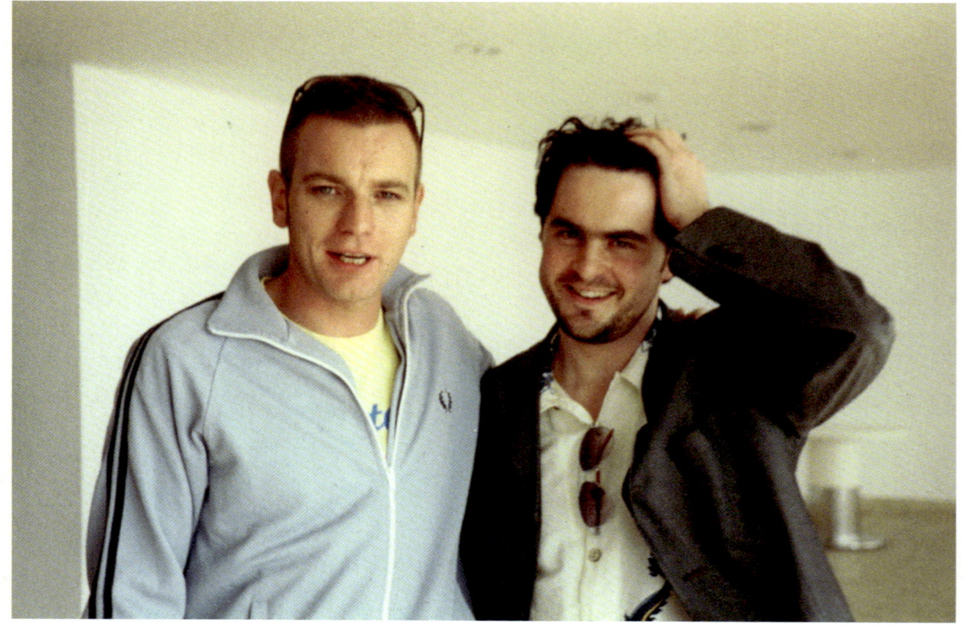

M 6

# 117. McTIERNAN, John

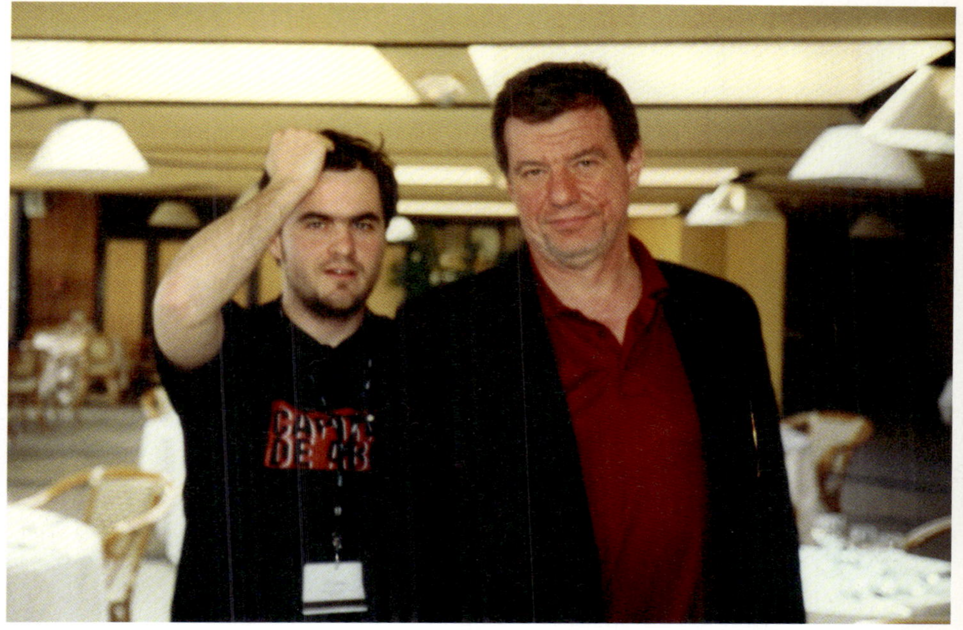

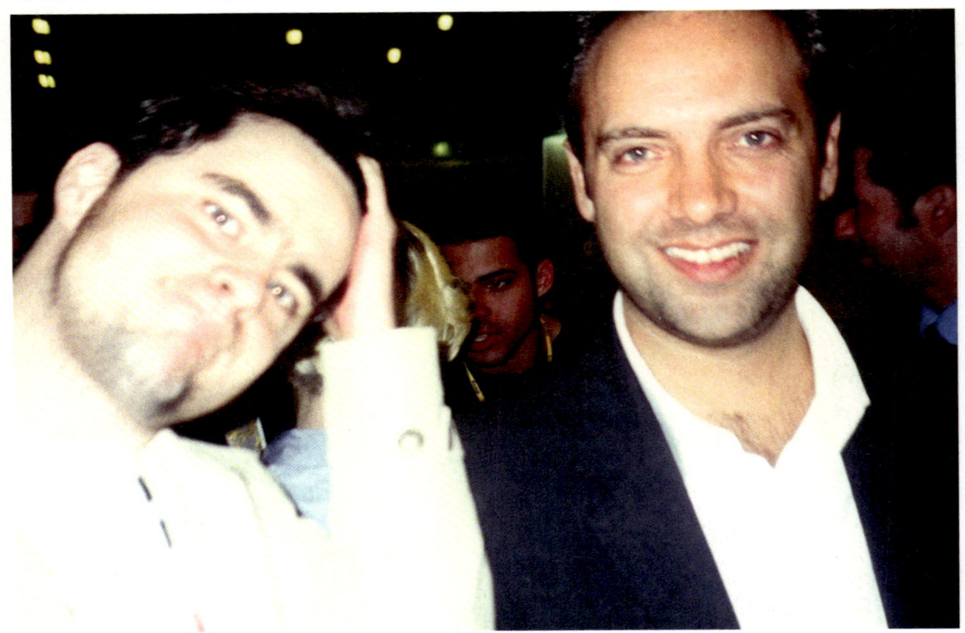

# 119. MENESES, Inês

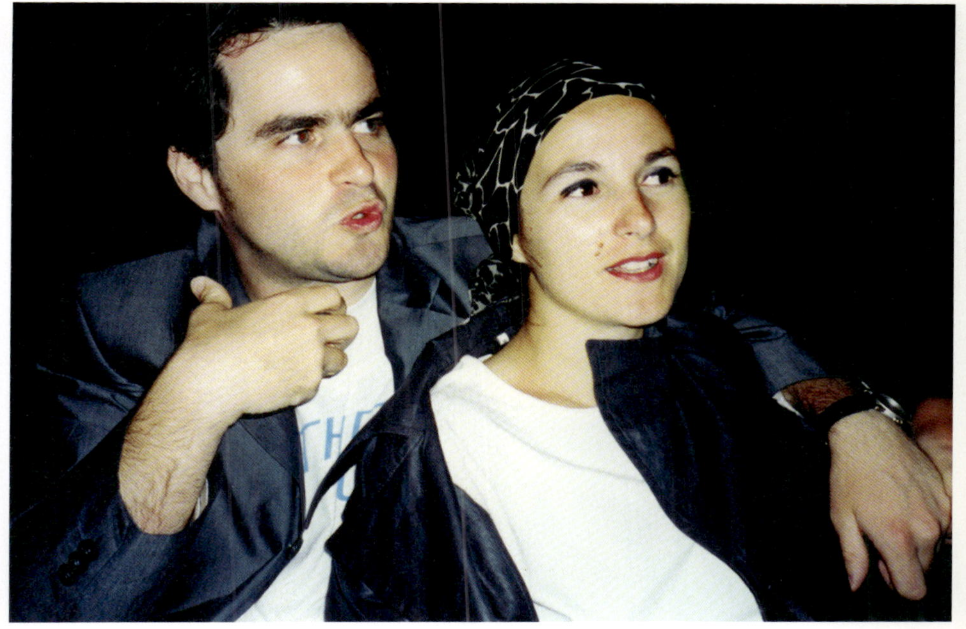

M 9

# 120. MIKKELSEN, Mads

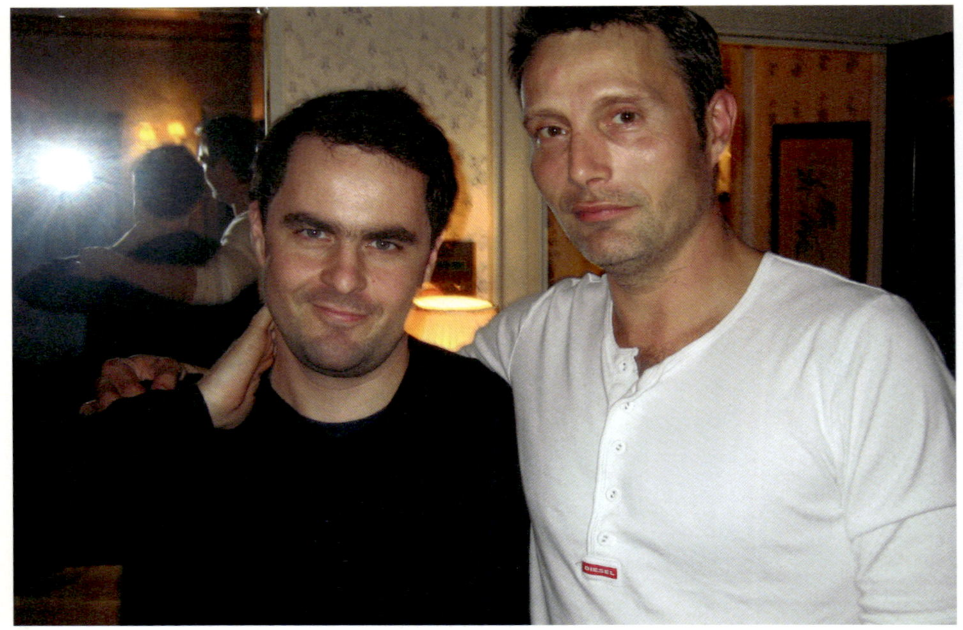

**M 10**

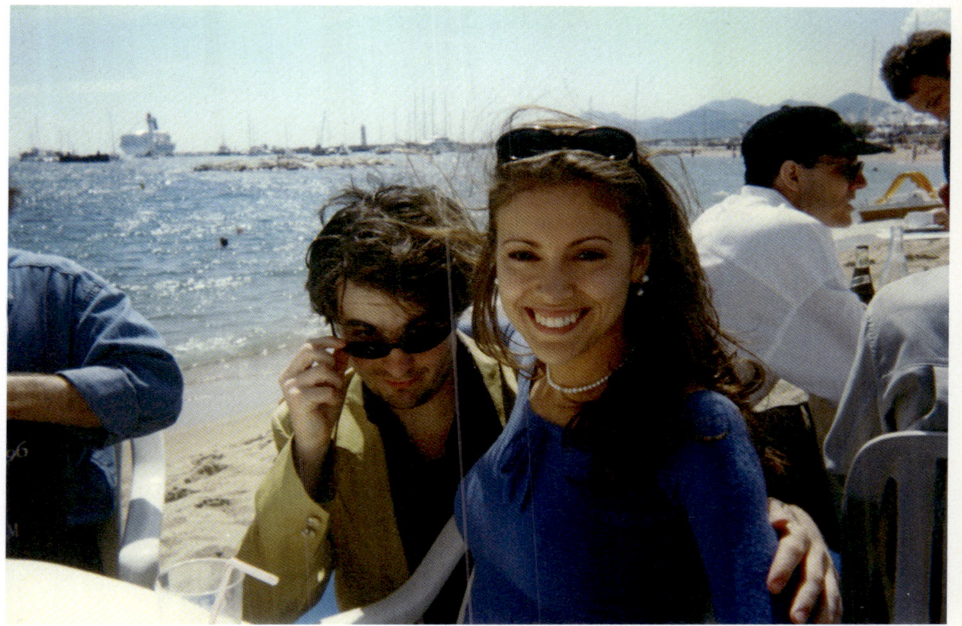

# 122. MOLKO, Brian

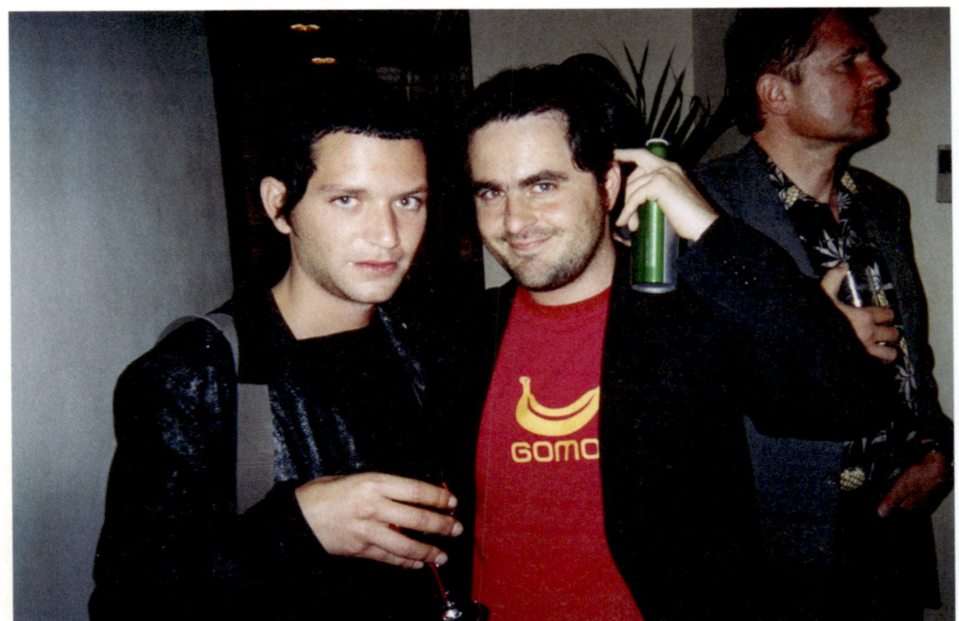

M 12

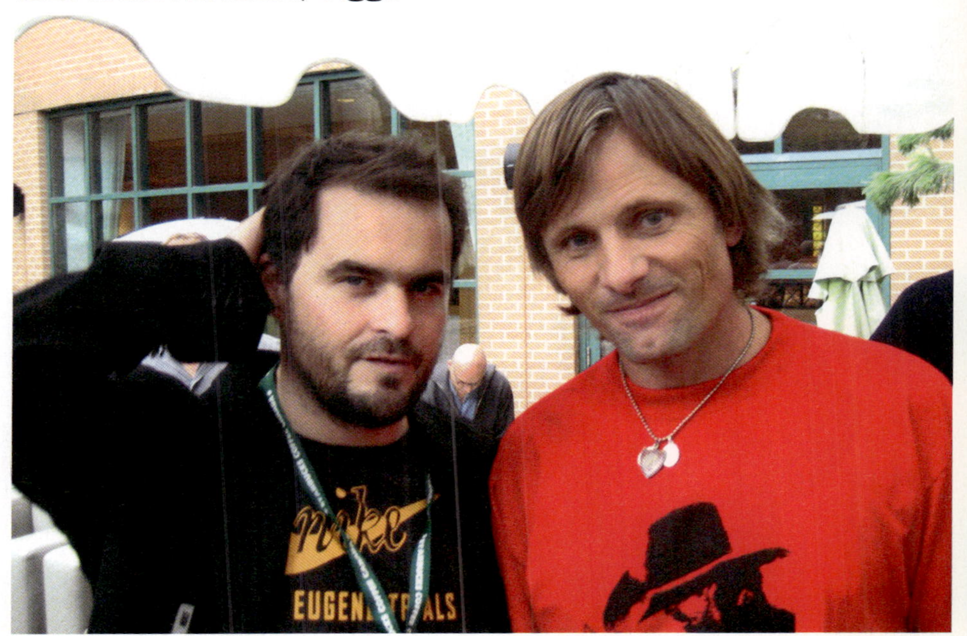

M 13

# 124. MURINO, Caterina

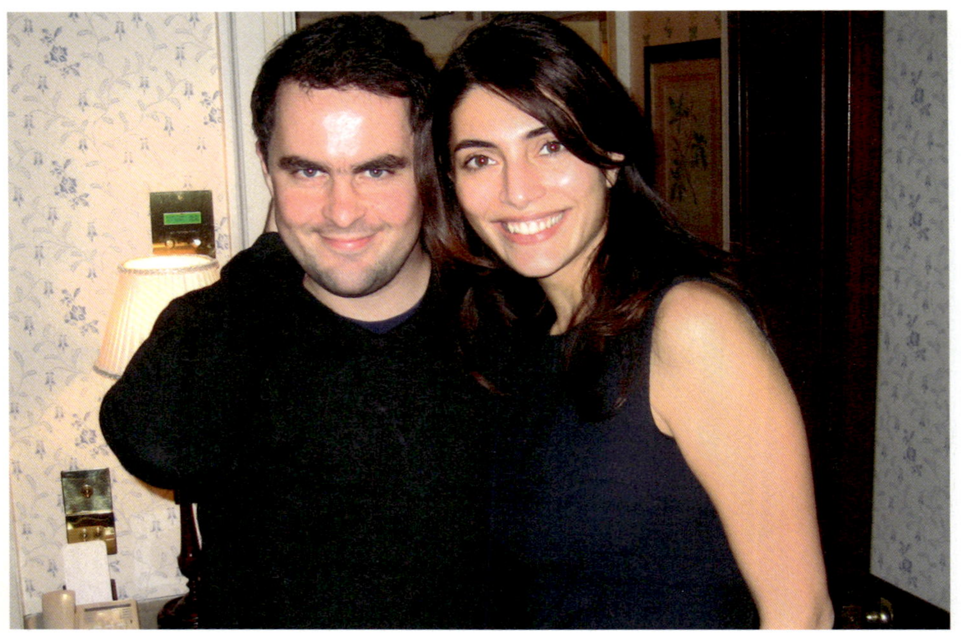

M 14

# 125. MYERS, Mike

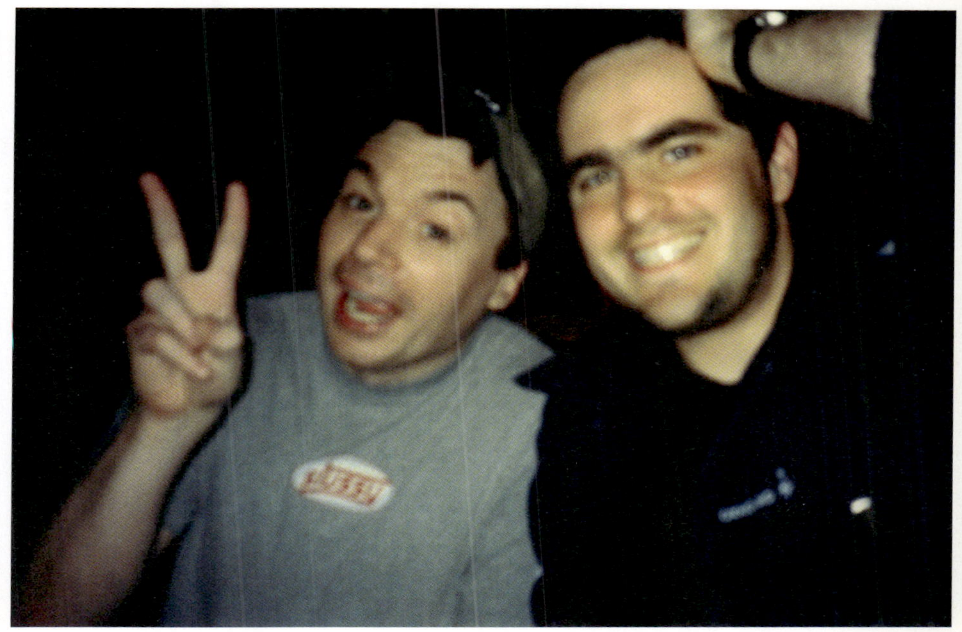

M 15

# 126. NACERI, Samy

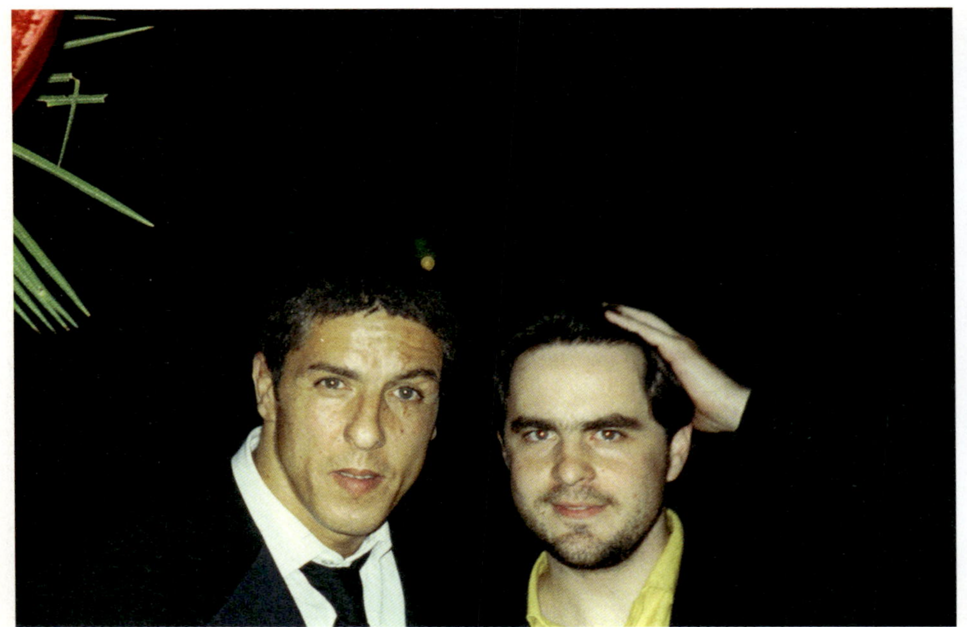

N 1

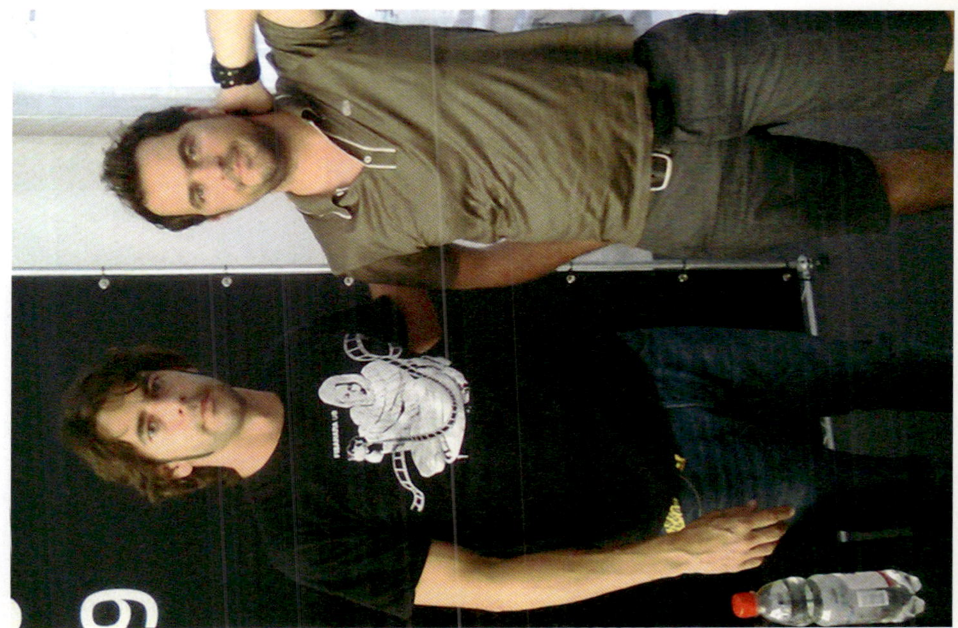

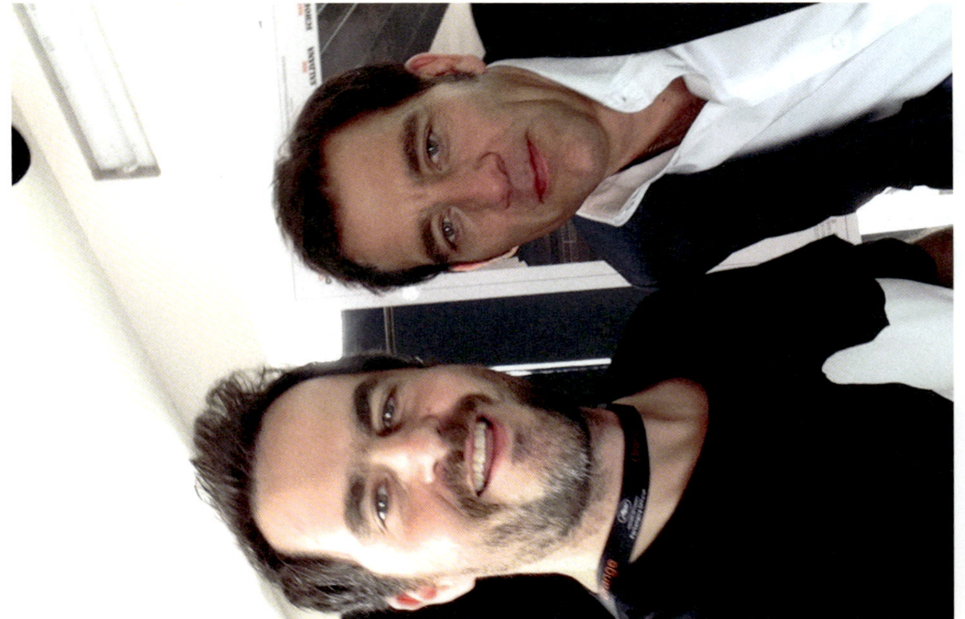

# 129. PARKER, Sarah Jessica

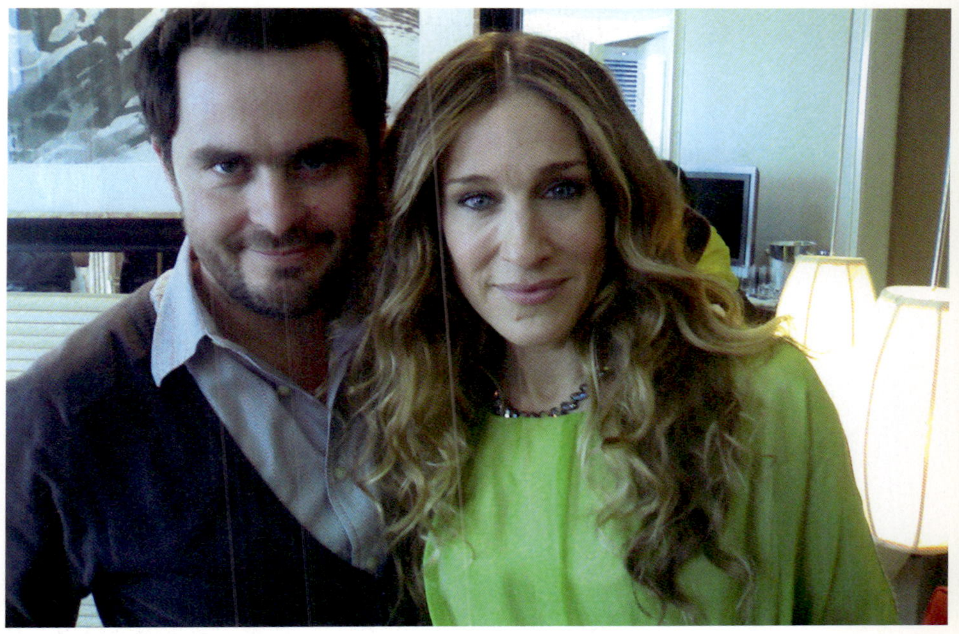

P 1

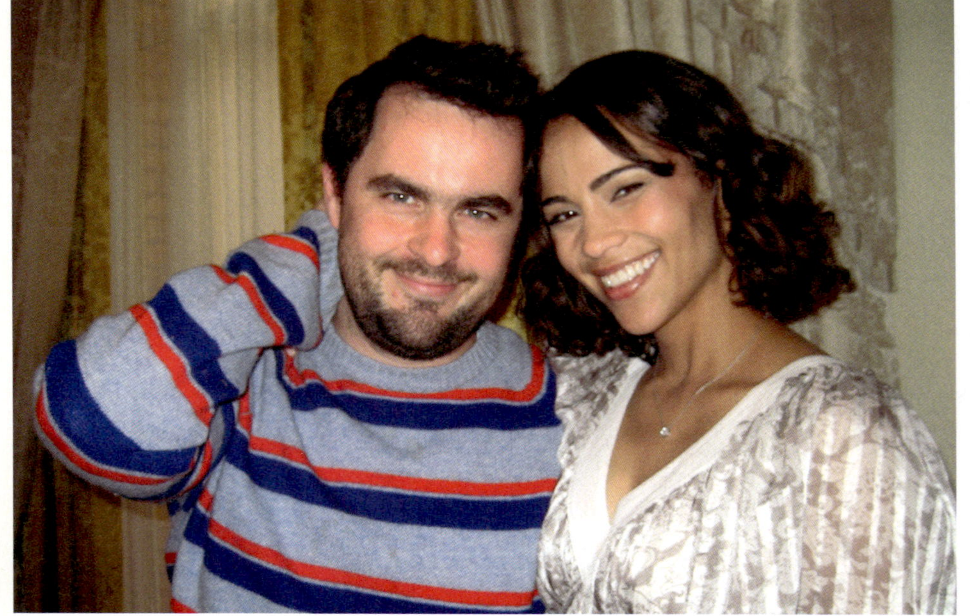

# 131. PEKAR, Harvey

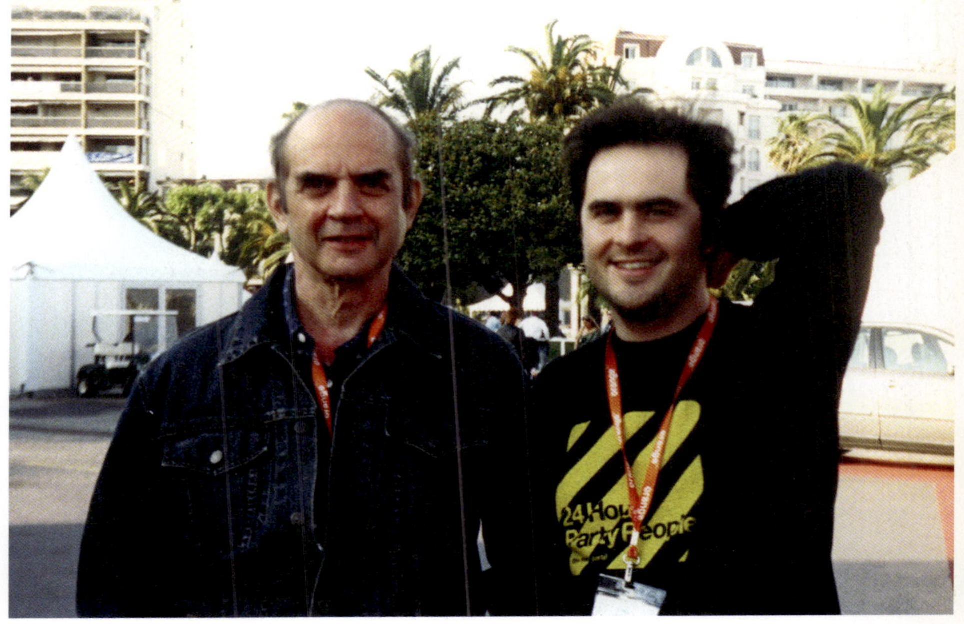

# 132. PEPPER, Barry

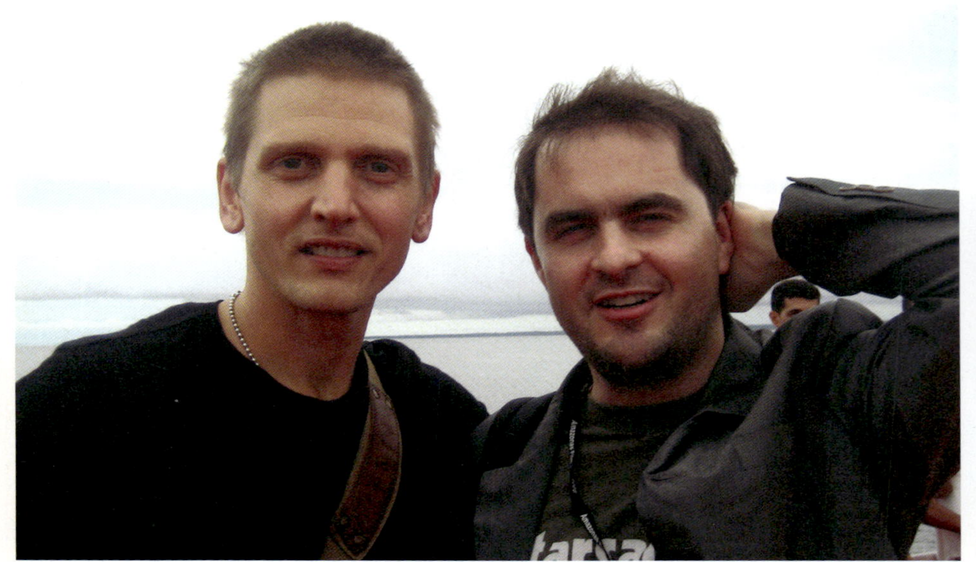

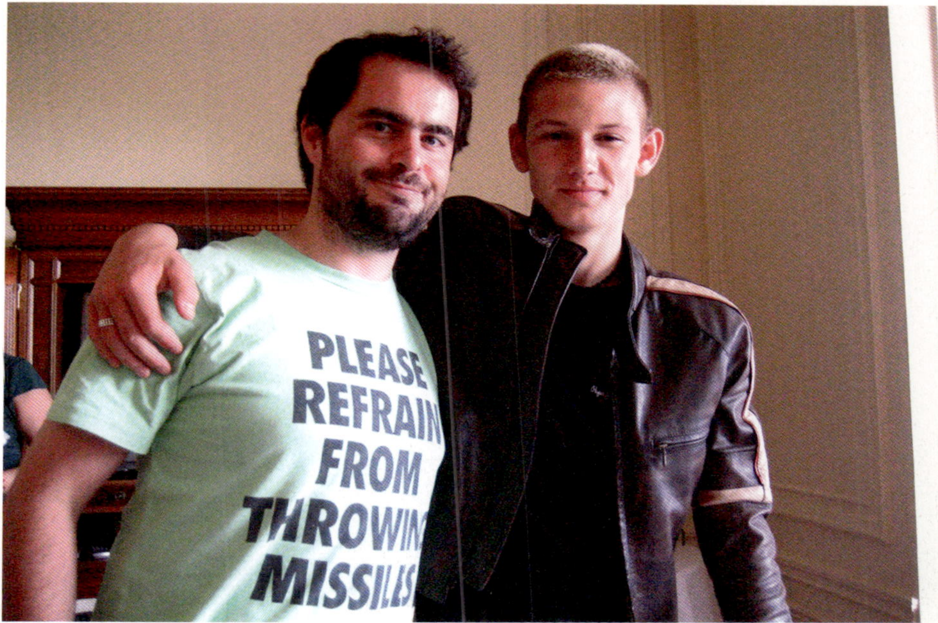

PLEASE
REFRAIN
FROM
THROWIN
MISSILES

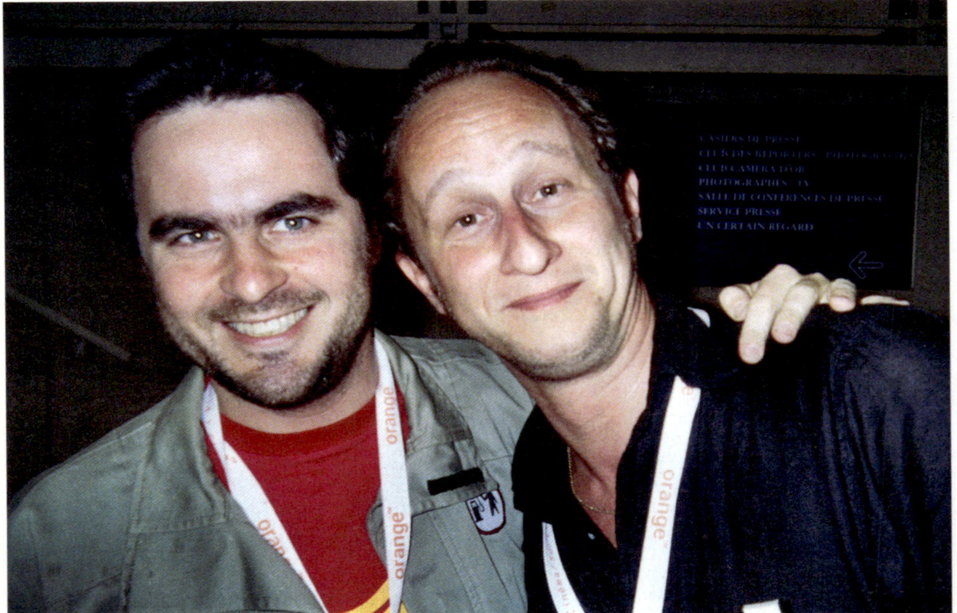
CASIERS DE PRESSE
CLUB DES REPORTERS PHOTOGRAPHES
CLUB CAMERA D'OR
PHOTOGRAPHIES TV
SALLE DE CONFERENCES DE PRESSE
SERVICE PRESSE
UN CERTAIN REGARD
orange
orange

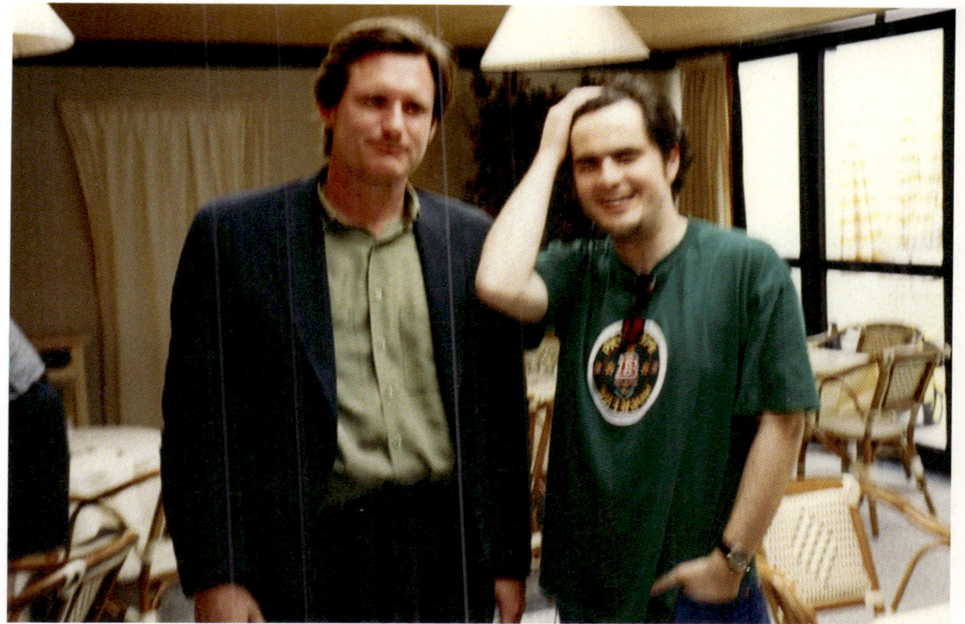

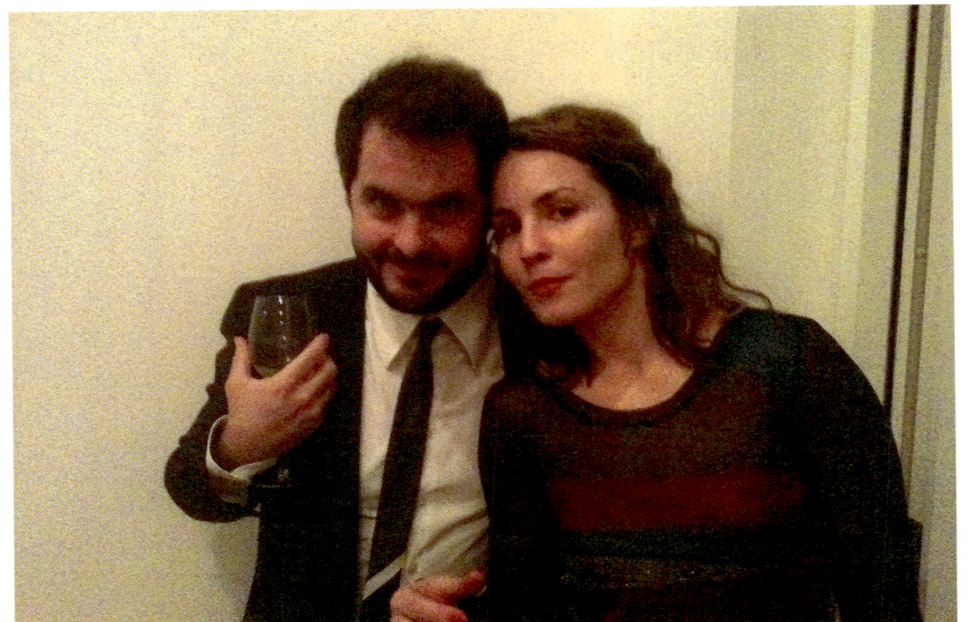

R 1

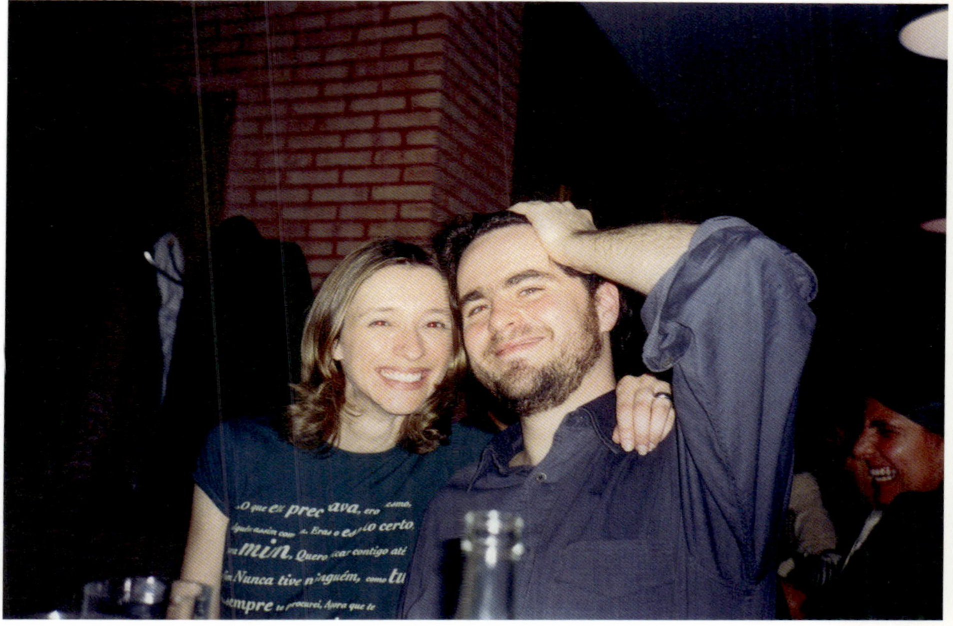
O que eu precisava, era como
alguém assim com... Eras o algo certo
min, Quero ficar contigo até
Nunca tive ninguém, como tu
sempre te procurei, Agora que te

# 138. REDGRAVE, Vanessa

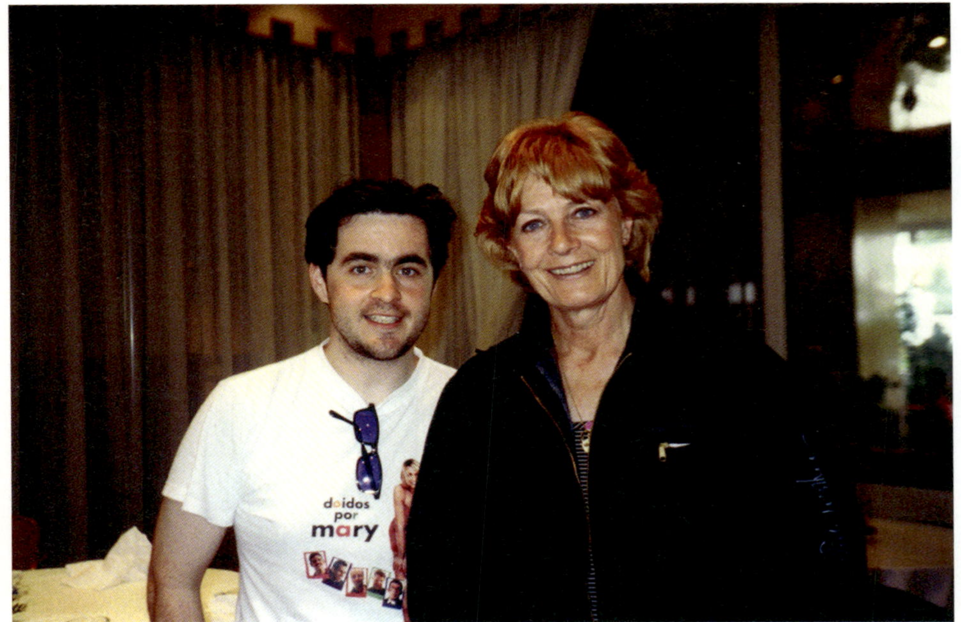

R 3

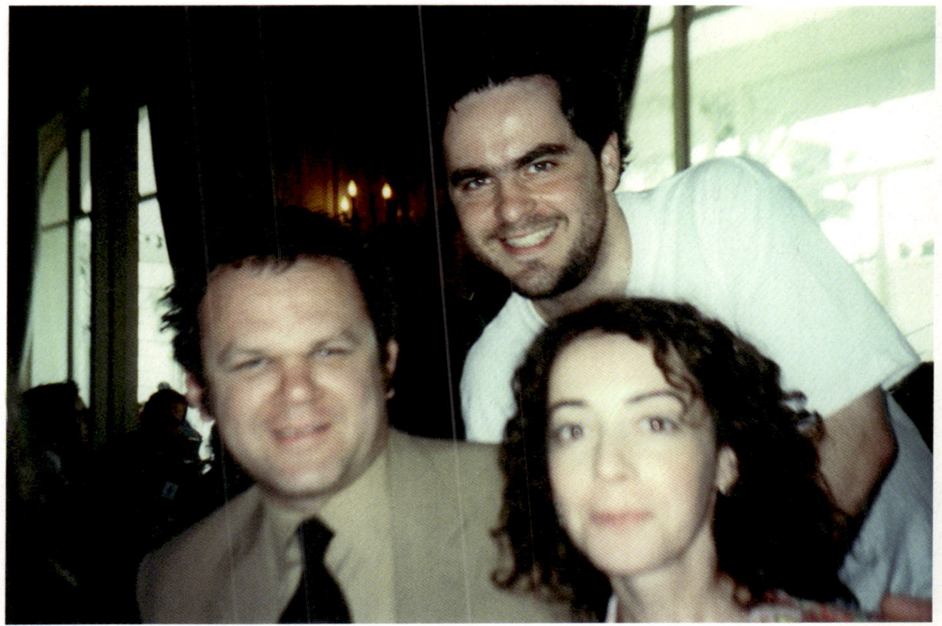

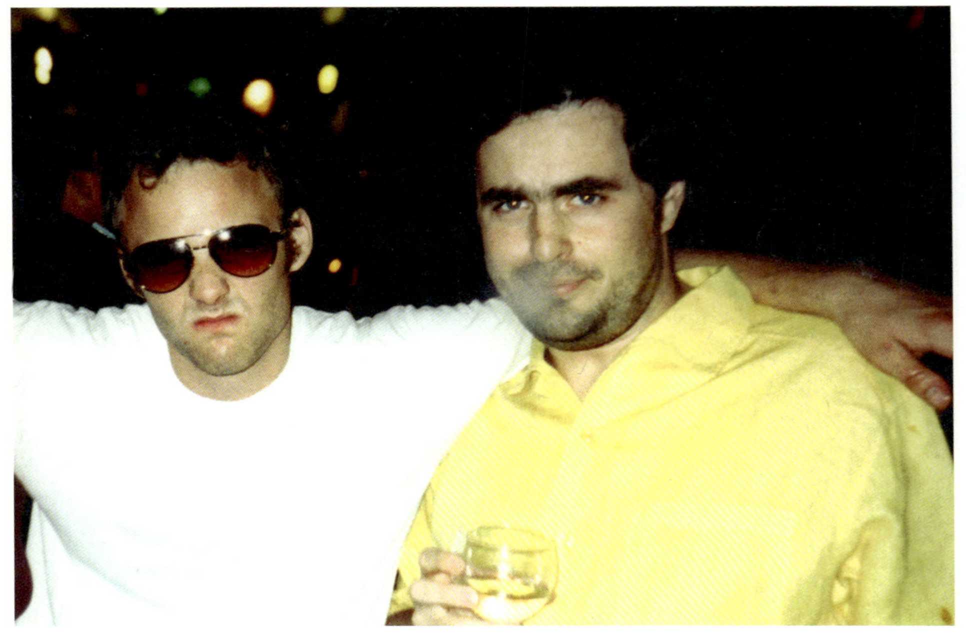

R 5

# 142. RHYS MEYERS, Jonathan

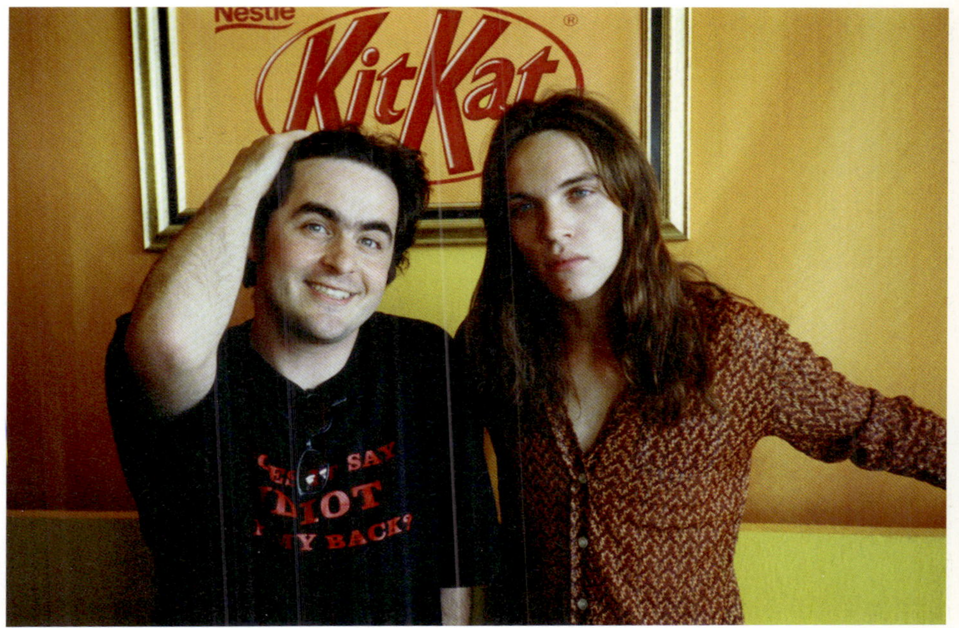

# 143. ROBBINS, Tim

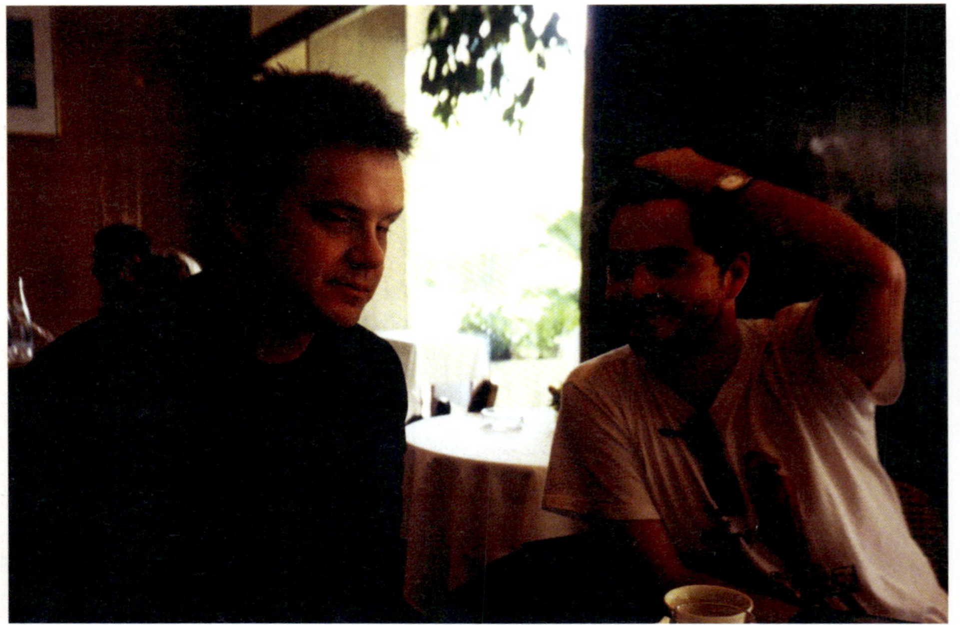

# 144. ROTH, Tim

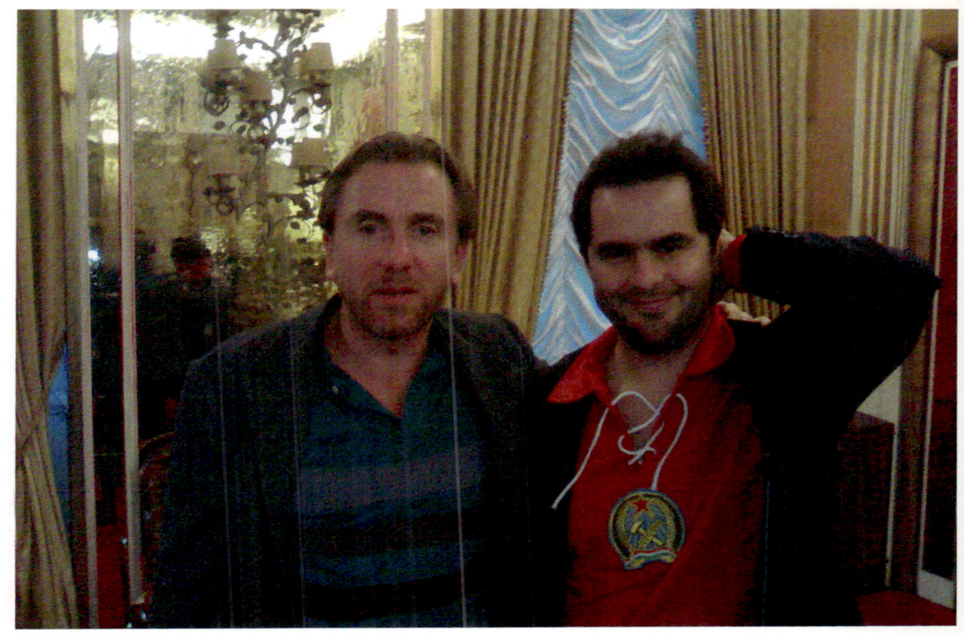

R 8

# 145. RUFFALO, Mark

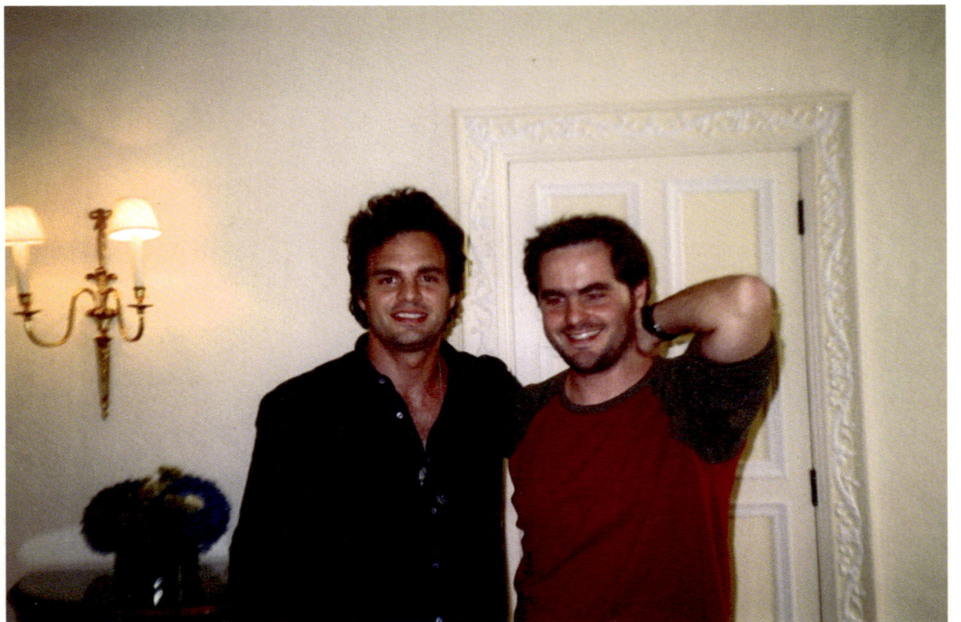

# 146. SAGNIER, Ludivine

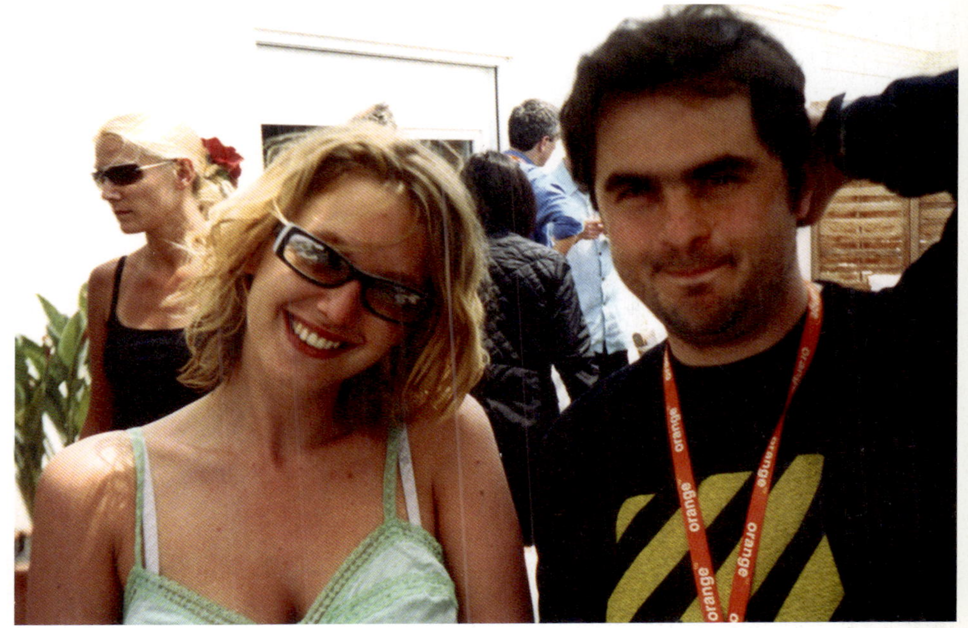

S 1

# 147. SANTOS, Lucélia

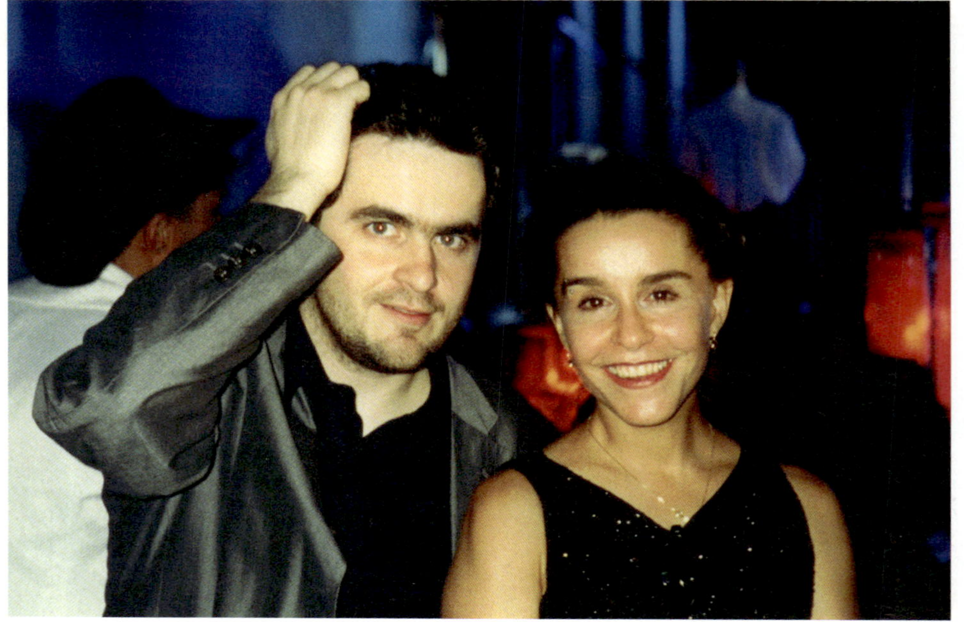

S 2

# 148. SEDGWICK, Kyra

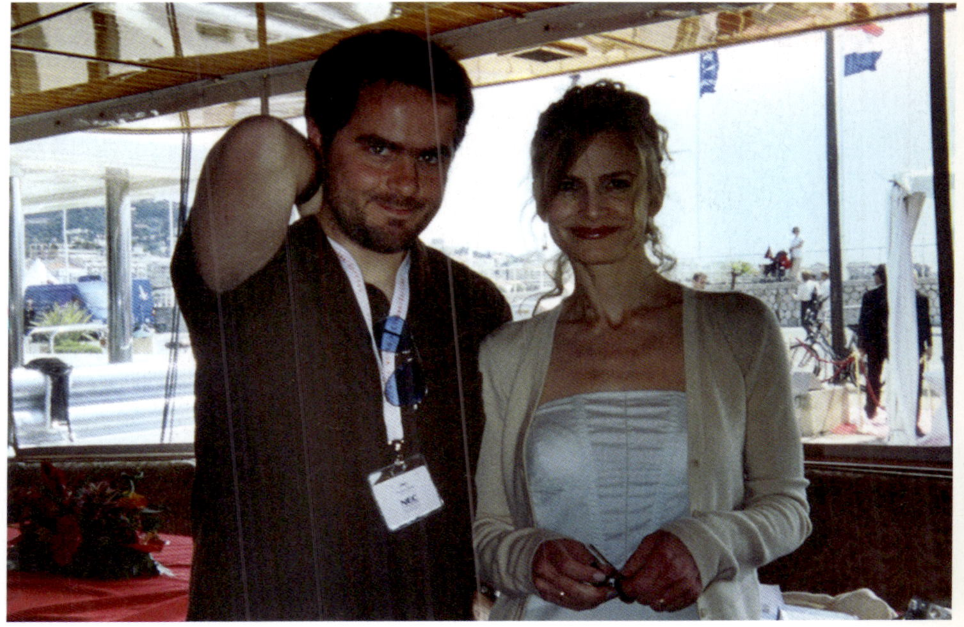

# 149. SEIGNER, Mathilde

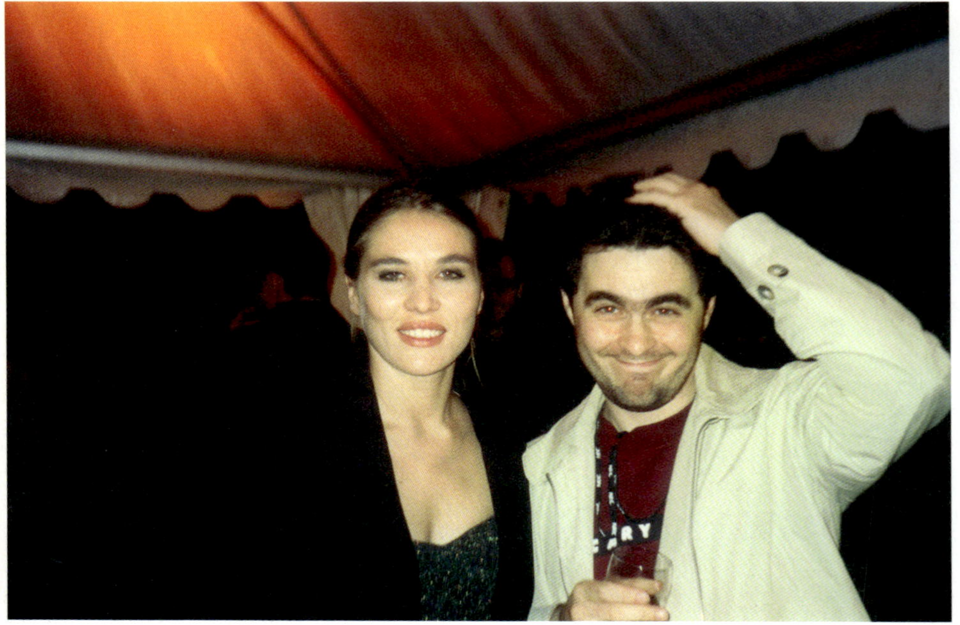

S 4

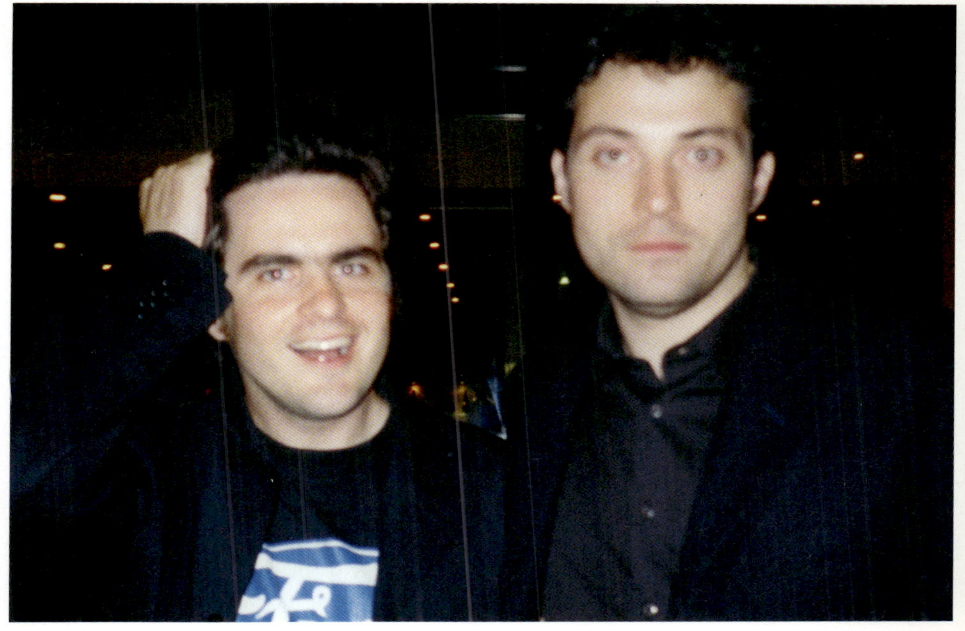

# 151. SMITH, Will

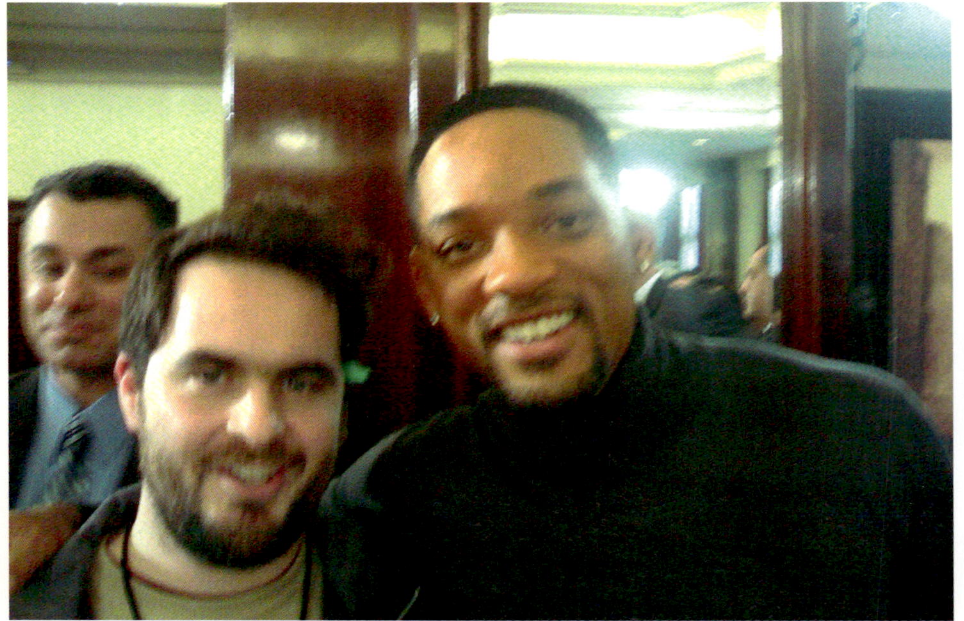

S 6

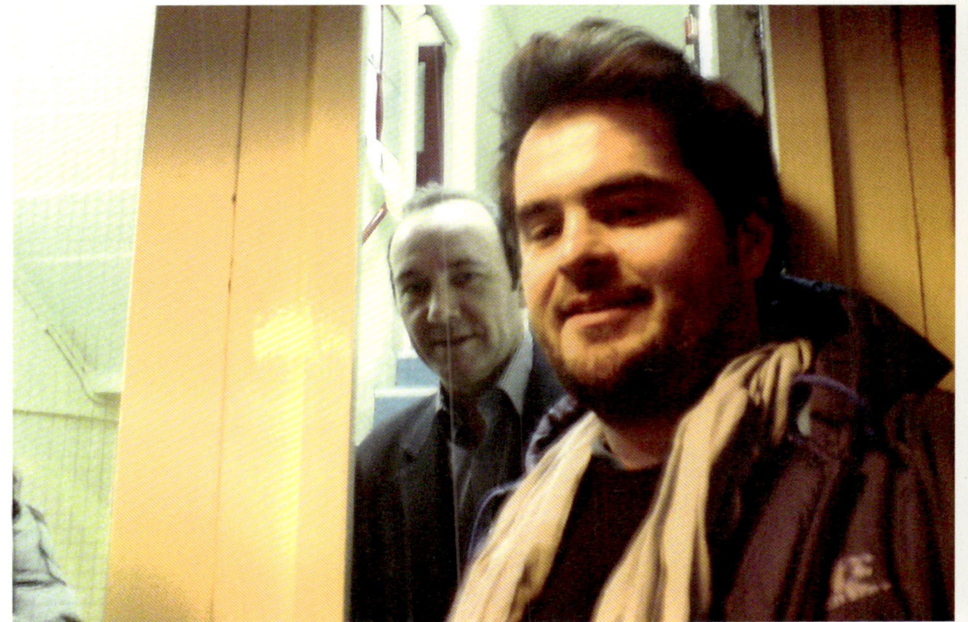

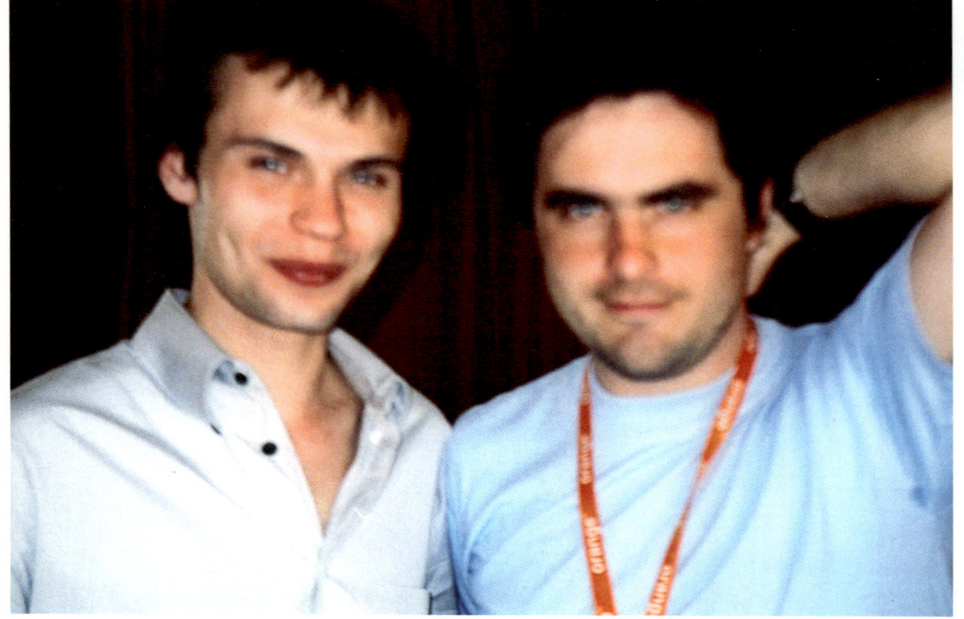

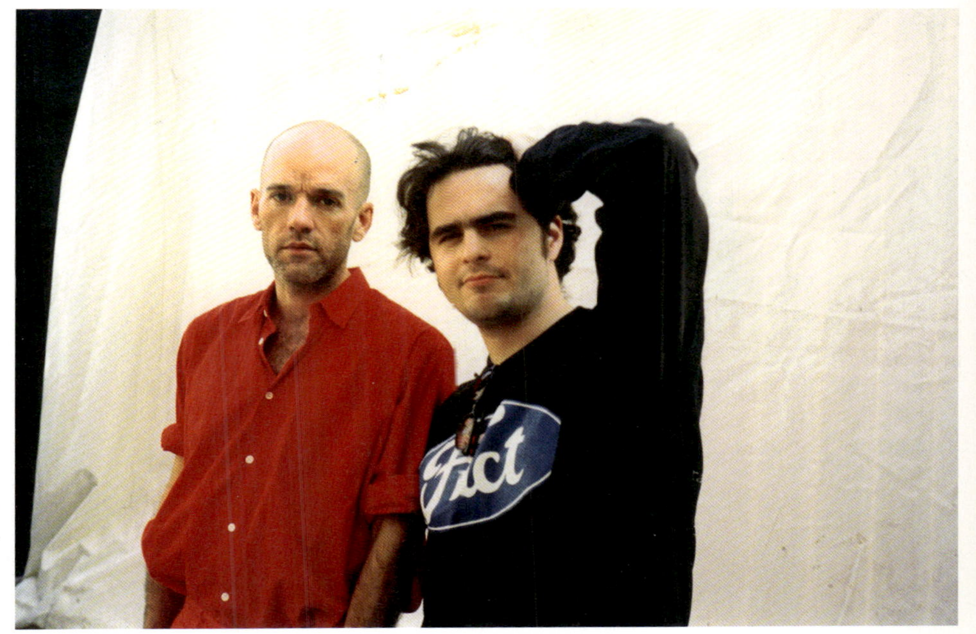
Fict

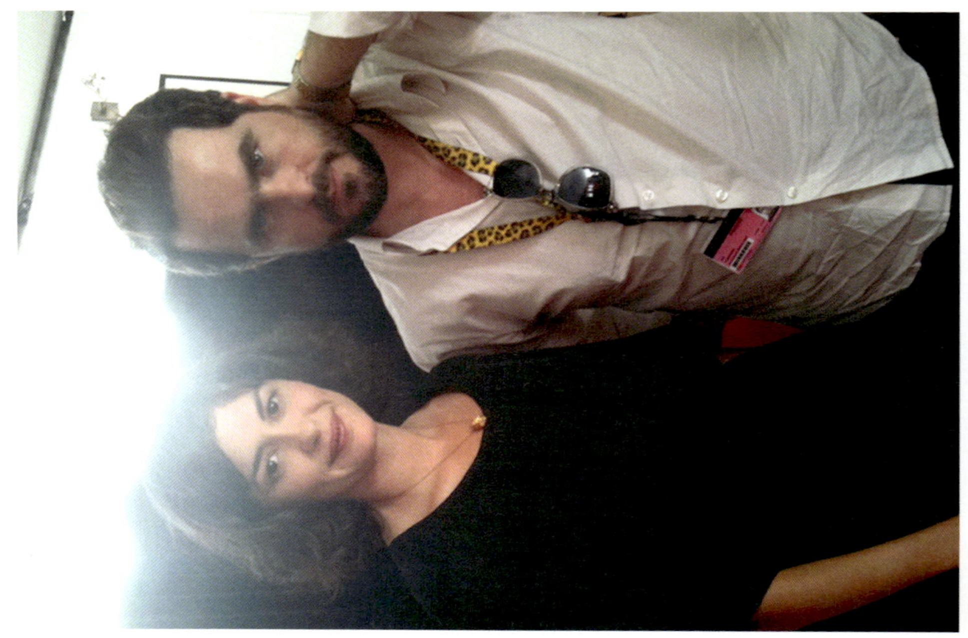

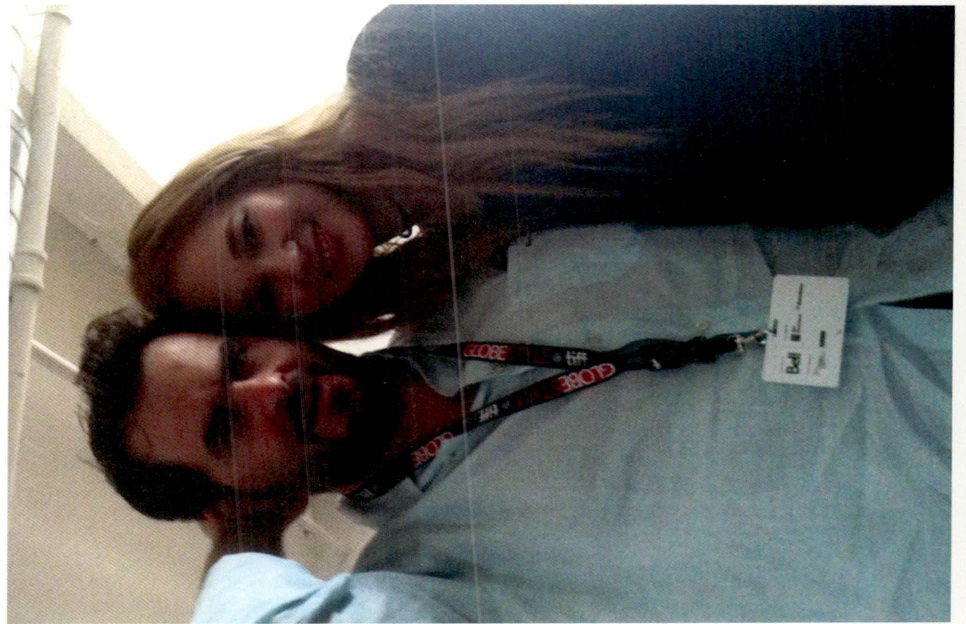



T 2

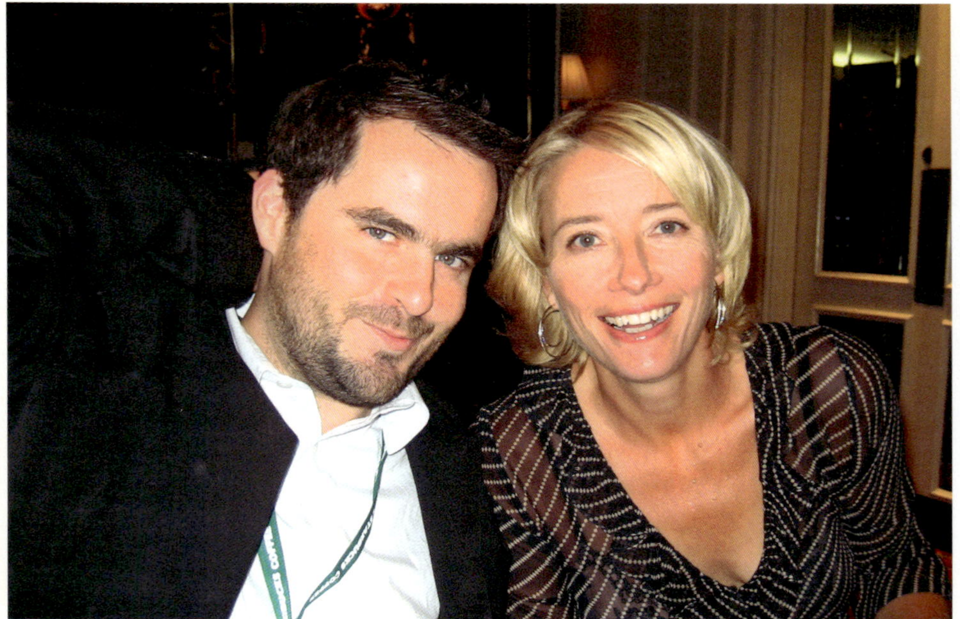

**T 3**

## 158. TUCKER, Chris

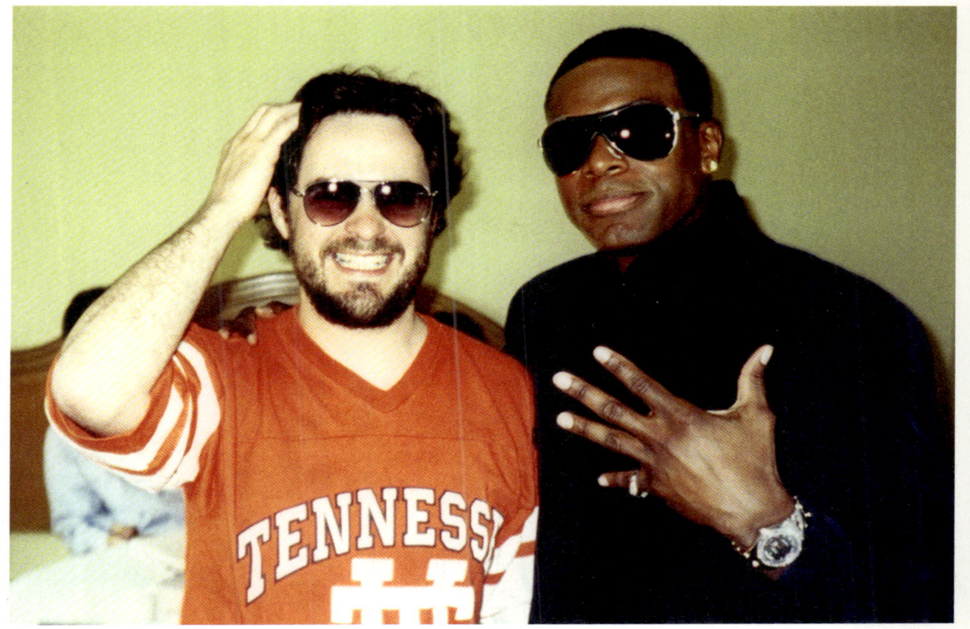

T 4

# 159. TURTURRO, John

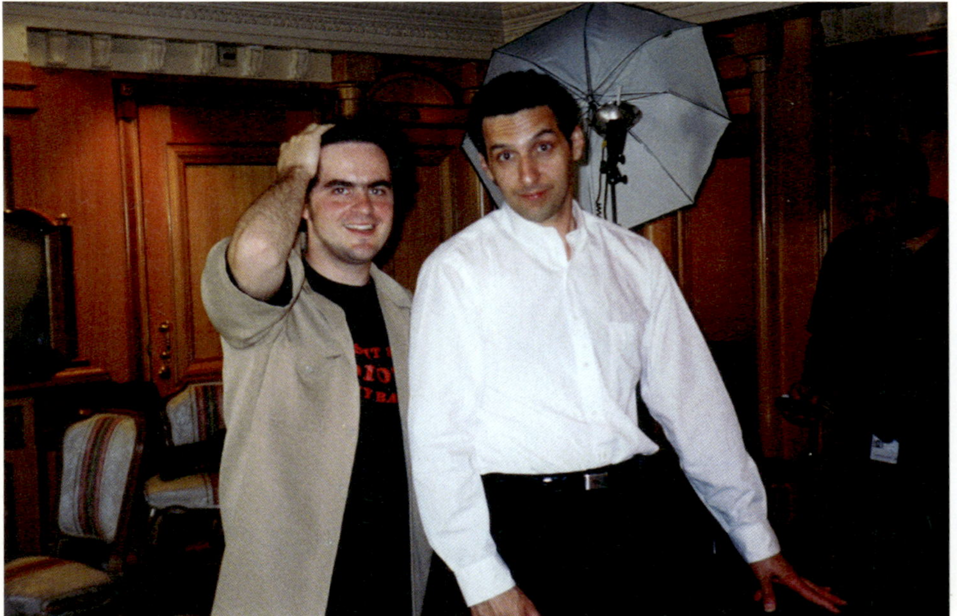

T 5

# 160. TYSON, Mike

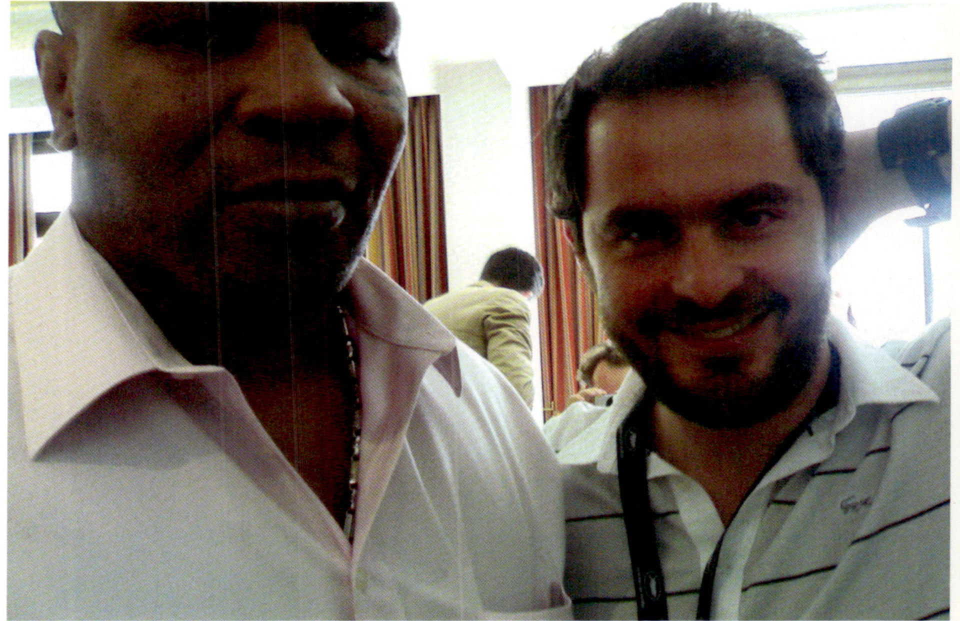

T 6

# 161. VAN HOUTEN, Carice

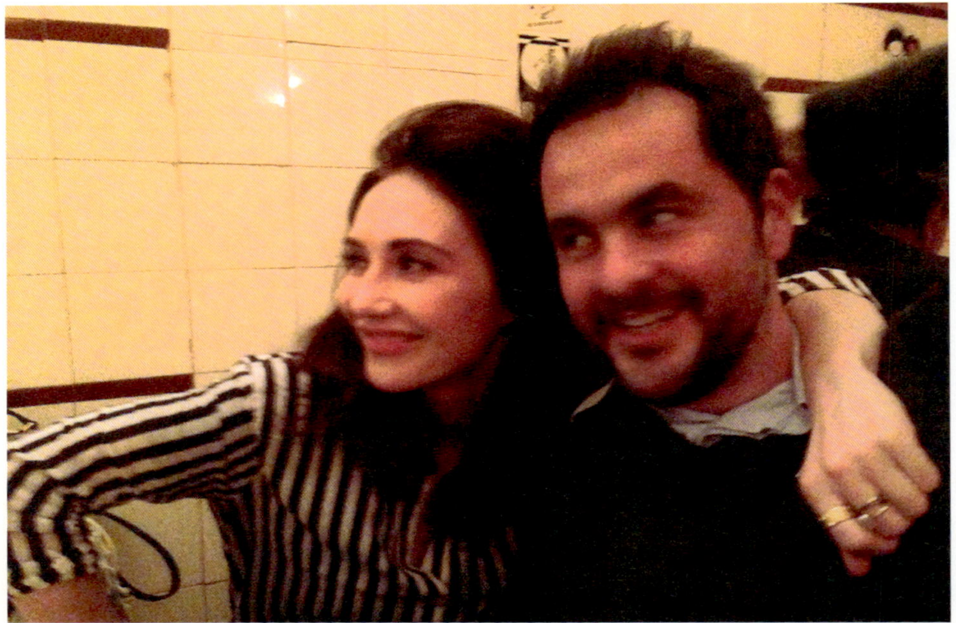

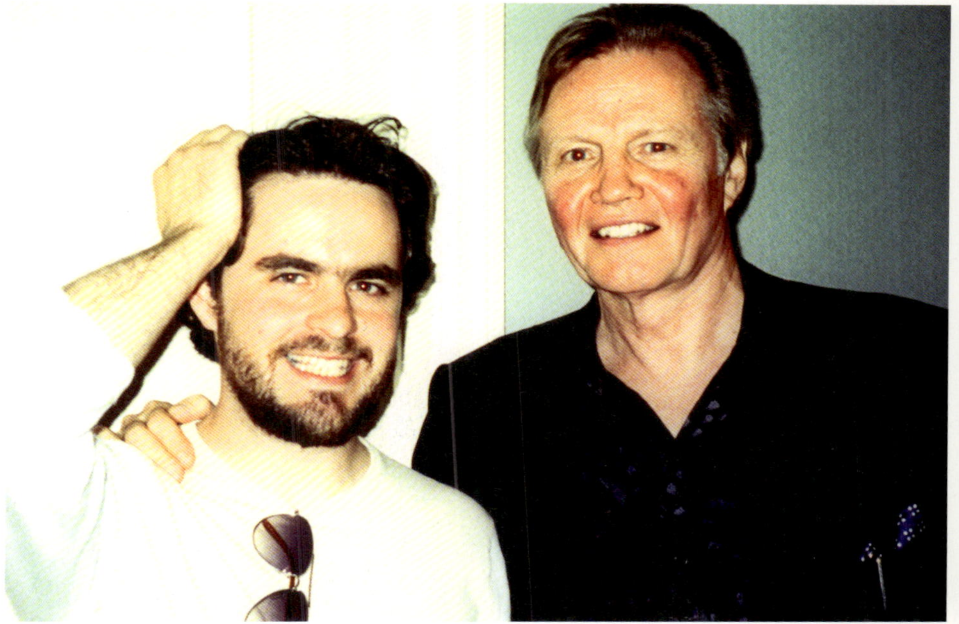

V 1

# 163. VON SYDOW, Max

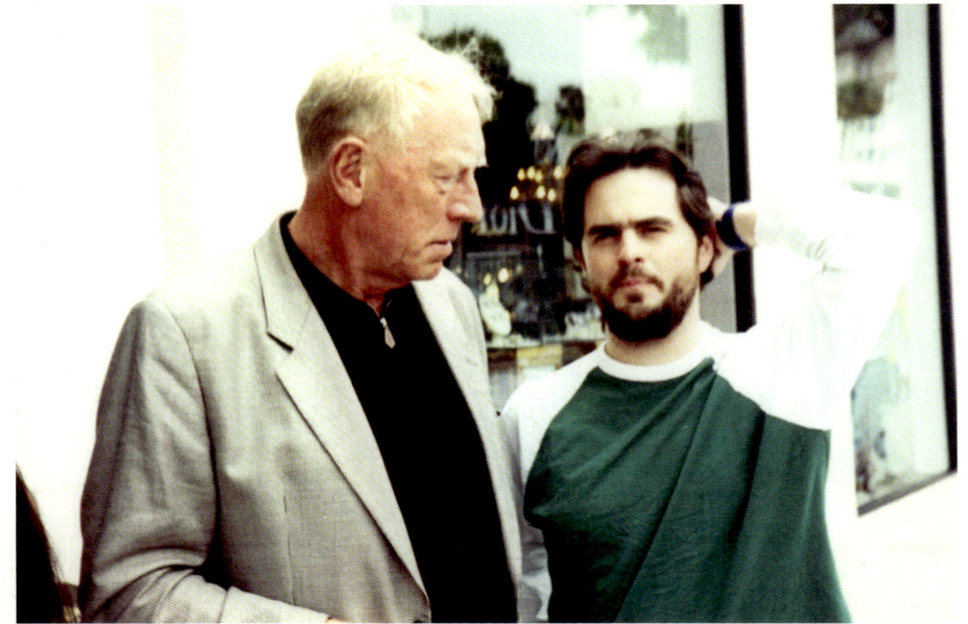

V 2

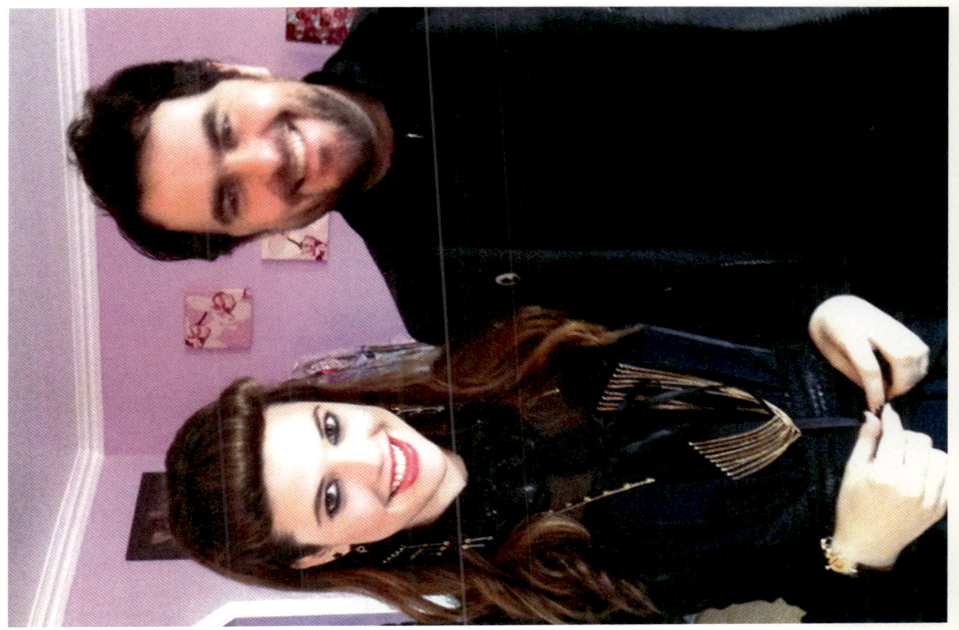

W 1

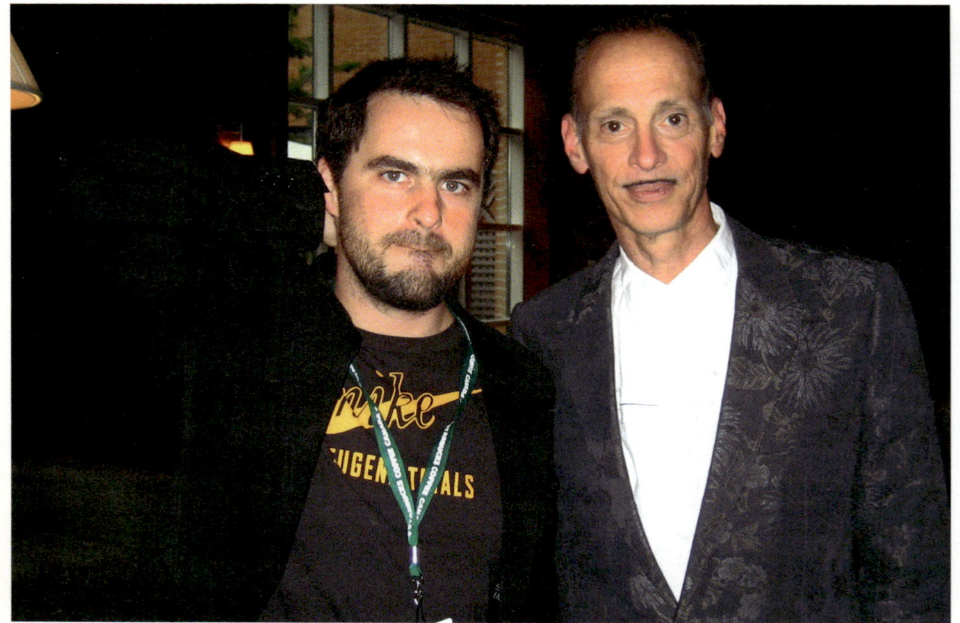

W 2

# 166. WATSON, Emily

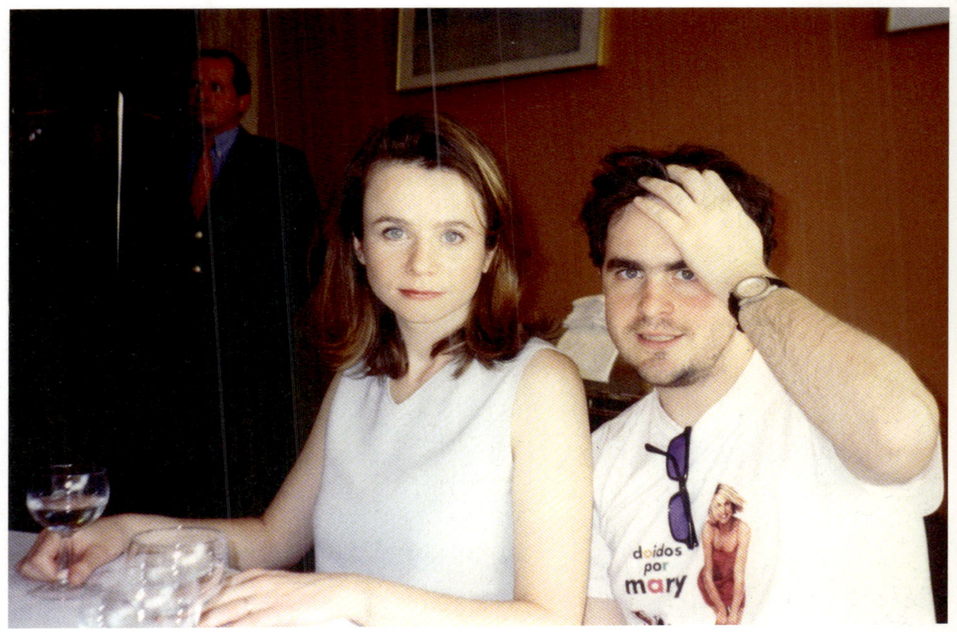

W 3

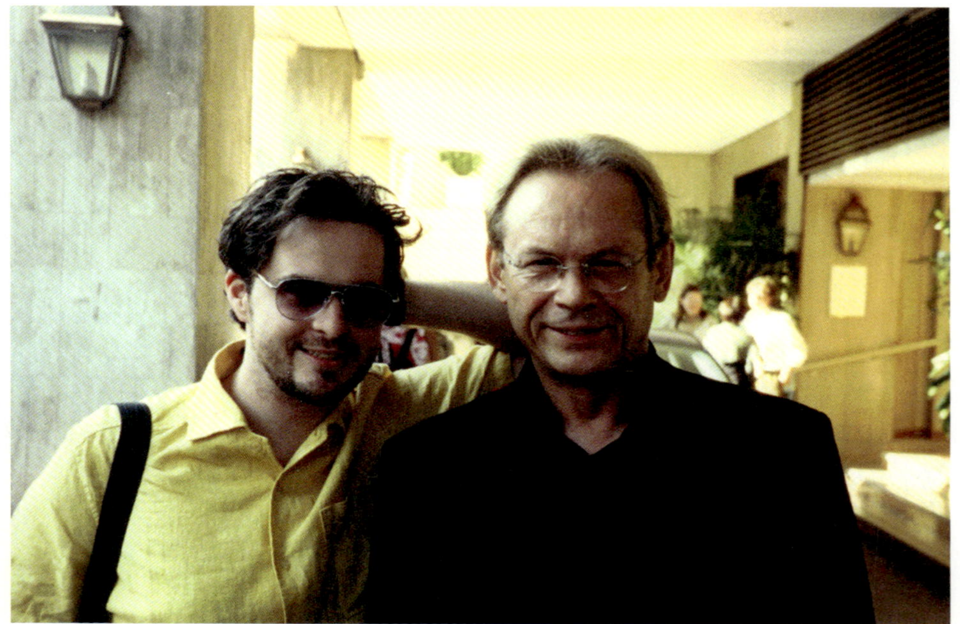

W 4

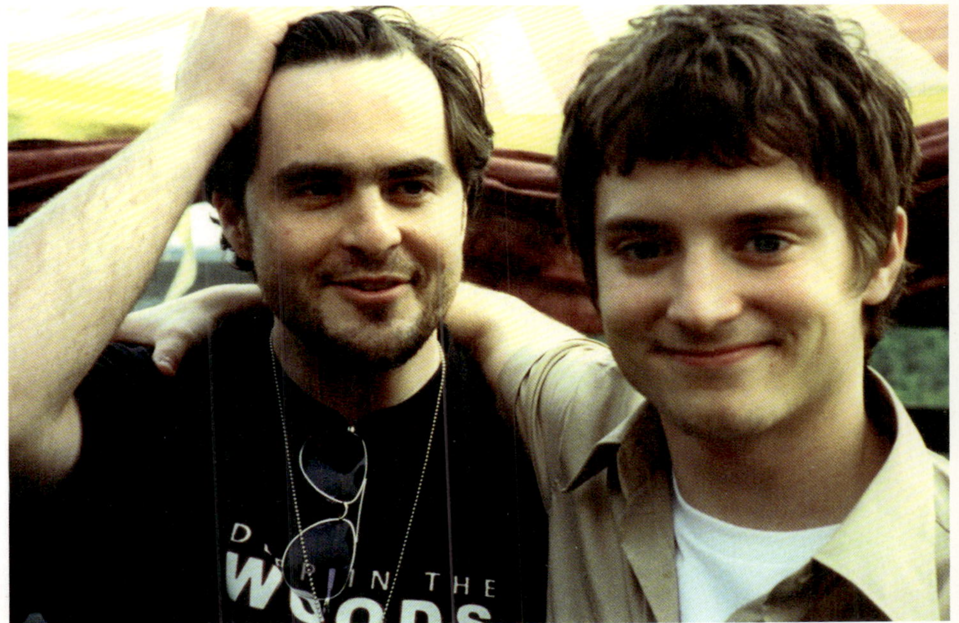


IN THE
WOODS

# 169. ZANE, Billy

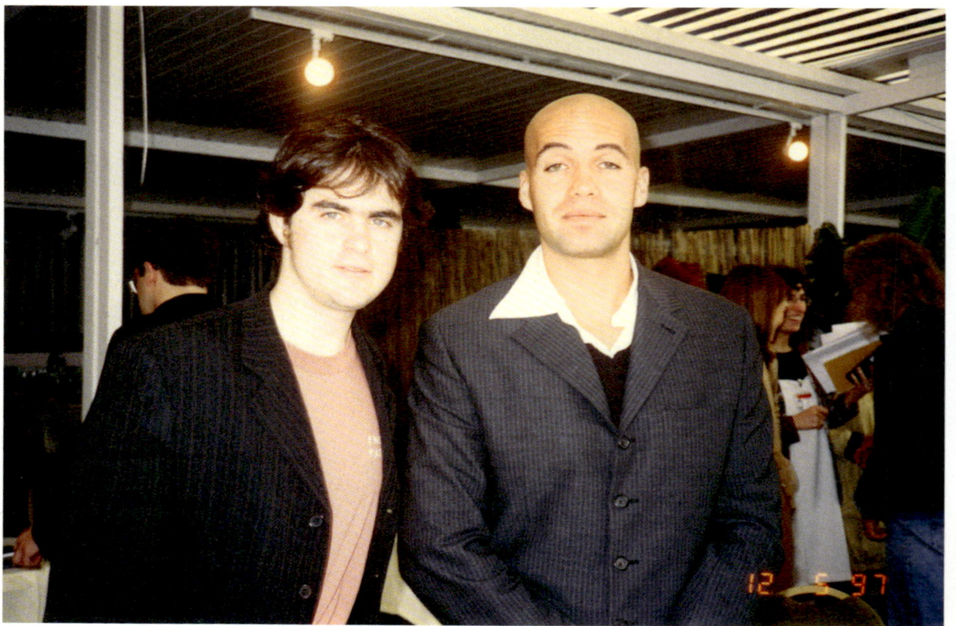

Z 1

# 170. ZHANG, Ziyi

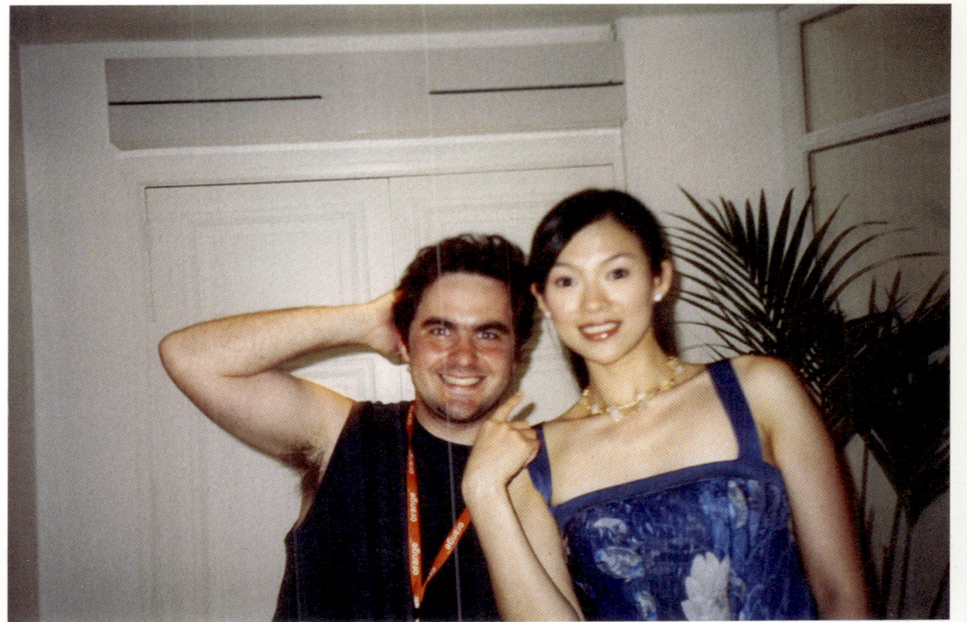

Z 2

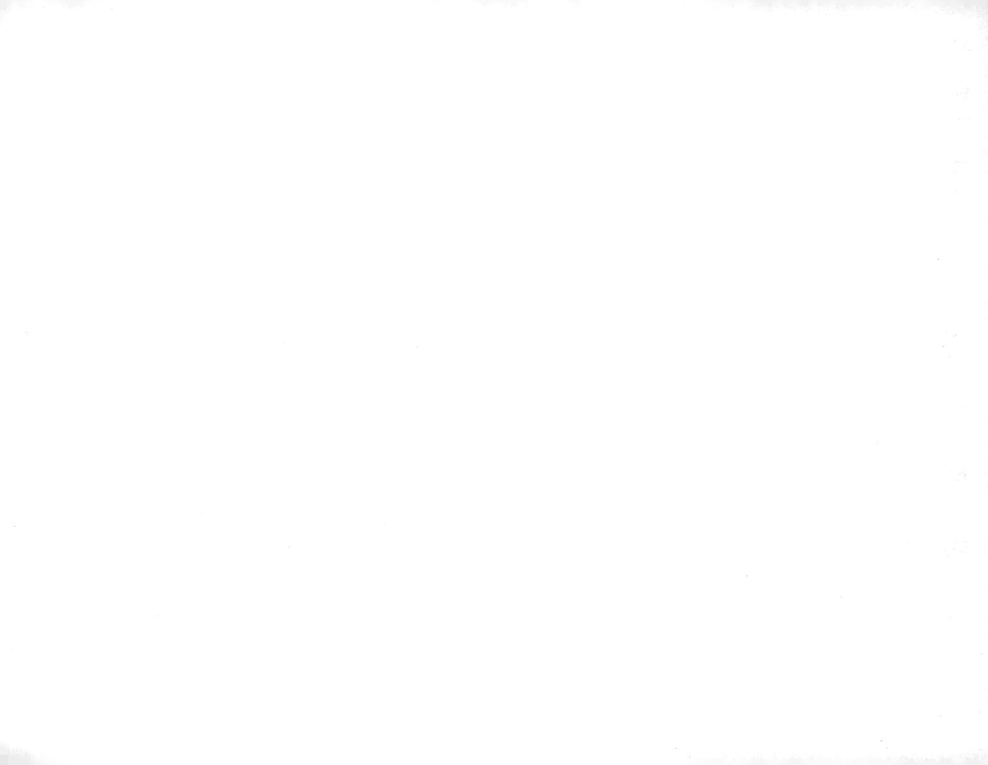

**COLOPHON**

From the archive of
Rui Pedro Tendinha

Design
Studio Luc Derycke, Ghent

Printed at
Lannoo, Tielt

Published by
MER. Paper Kunsthalle
Geldmunt 36
B-9000 Ghent
www.merpaperkunsthalle.org

© 2013 Julião Sarmento
© 2013 MER.

ISBN 978 94 9177 533 8
D/2013/7852/214